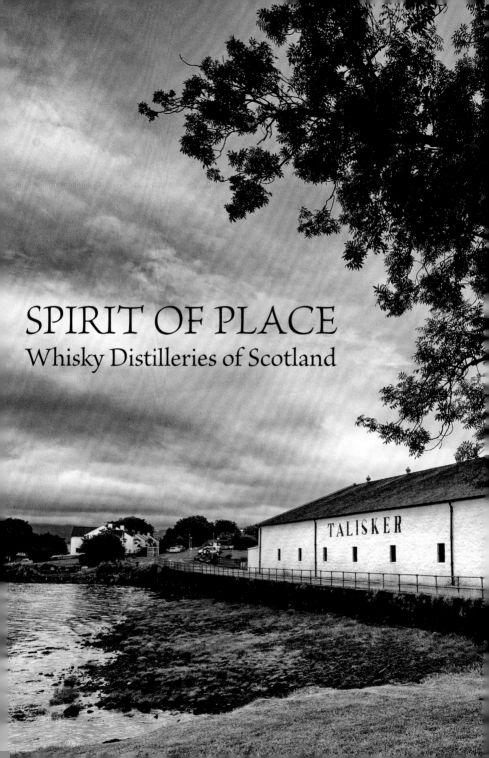

SPIRIT OF PLACE
Whisky Distilleries of Scotland

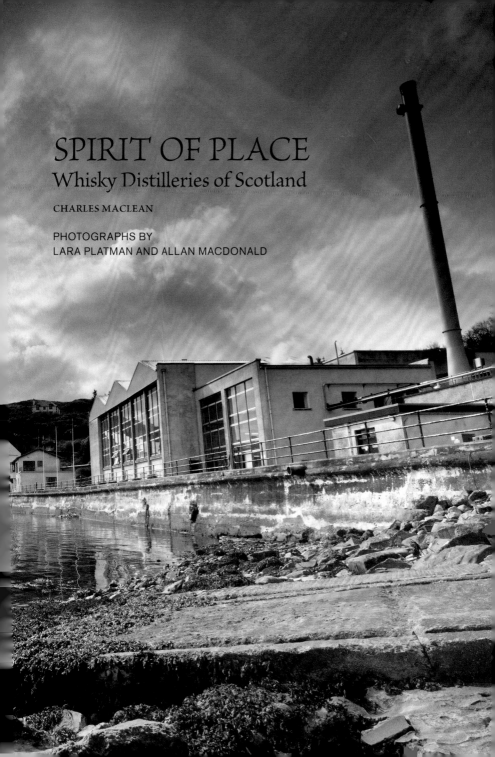

SPIRIT OF PLACE
Whisky Distilleries of Scotland

CHARLES MACLEAN

PHOTOGRAPHS BY
LARA PLATMAN AND ALLAN MACDONALD

Orkney
Islands

NORTH SEA

Lewis

North
Highlands

Outer Hebrides

Speyside

Skye

East
Highlands

Inner Hebrides

Central
Highlands

West
Highlands

Mull

SCOTLAND

Jura

Lowlands ■Edinburgh

Islay

Isle of
Arran

CONTENTS

Introduction   6

1: LOWLANDS
Auchentoshan   14
Glenkinchie   18
Daftmill   22

2: ISLAY
Ardbeg   28
Bowmore   32
Bruichladdich   34
Bunnahabhain   38
Caol Ila   42
Kilchoman   44
Lagavulin   48
Laphroaig   50

3: CENTRAL HIGHLANDS
Aberfeldy   56
Blair Athol   60
Dalwhinnie   64
Deanston   68
Edradour   72
Glengoyne   76
Glenturret   80
Tomatin   84
Tullibardine   88

4: NORTH HIGHLANDS
Balblair   94
Clynelish   96
Dalmore   100
Glenmorangie   102
Glen Ord   108
Old Pulteney   112
Wolfburn   114

5: EAST HIGHLANDS
Fettercairn   120
Glendronach   122
Glen Garioch   126
Knockdhu   130
Royal Lochnagar   136

6: WEST HIGHLANDS
Ben Nevis   140
Oban   144
Springbank   146

7: SPEYSIDE
Aberlour   154
Aultmore   158
The Balvenie   162
BenRiach   166
Benromach   170
Cardhu   174
Cragganmore   178
Glenfarclas   182
Glenfiddich   186
Glen Grant   192
The Glenlivet   196
Glen Moray   200
Glenrothes   204
Knockando   208
Macallan   212
Strathisla   216
Tamdhu   220

8: THE ISLANDS
Abhainn Dearg   224
Isle of Arran   230
Highland Park   234
Jura   238
Scapa   242
Talisker   244
Tobermory   248

Index   252
Credits   256

INTRODUCTION

I have long maintained that malt whisky is the quintessence of Scotland. For me, it conjures the land of its birth in all its seasons with every sip – flowering machair in spring, warm beaches and heather pollen in summer, wayside berries and orchards in autumn, and the reek of winter peat ('reek' here being the term distillers use to describe peat smoke). The smells of cooking and baking, childhood sweets, leather upholstery, grandpa's motor car, church candles, cut grass, meadows, pine forests, sawn timber... the aromas called to mind are rich indeed.

The associations I make are necessarily personal and are usually associated with smell rather than taste. It is well known that, of all our senses, smell most rapidly and effectively stirs long-term memory, but with a little imagination, the images arise like friendly phantoms to enhance my appreciation of the dram in my glass.

As my friend, the songwriter Robin Laing, puts it in one of his songs: 'It's the pulse of one small nation – so much more than just a dram – [evoking] the people and the weather and the land: the past distilled into the present.'

Another friend once said: 'When you buy a bottle of whisky you are buying an awful lot more than "liquor in a bottle". You are buying history and high craft; tradition and experience;

all the time that has gone into the making and the maturing.'

Malt whisky does more than evoke the place in which it is made – it arises from it. According to whisky philosopher Dave Broom, 'Scotland's landscape has formed the industry in multifarious ways, from dictating where distilleries could be built, offering places to hide and then places to prosper... There is even the tantalising possibility that early distillers tried to capture the vivid scents of hot gorse, fresh flowers, heather and bracken in their whiskies.' He describes this as 'cultural terroir.' Elsewhere he expands the notion, explaining that life in the Highlands is a compromise 'between man and land,' and suggests that many fail in their enterprises because they forget that the land has the upper hand. Whisky, however, has survived and continues to thrive because it is pragmatic. Broom says that it is as though the distillery workers have concluded that whisky making is something that they *can* do in this environment and what's more, 'because we have done it for generations it reflects where we are, who we are and what we make.'

It is an interesting concept. When French winemakers use the term *terroir*, they do so to describe the profound influence of geography, climate and geology upon the flavour, style and quality of their wines

– ultimately to describe the very soil in which their grapes grow. The concept cannot be applied in precisely the same way to whisky distilling, but it does appear that somehow the subtle influences of local geography, combined with tradition, process and plant, act to differentiate the whisky made in each distillery and every region of Scotland, in ways that are still not fully understood by science.

Regional differences

In the 1980s it became common to discuss malt whiskies in terms of 'regional differences', on the basis that the malts made in one part of Scotland are different to those made in another. This was really no more than a brilliant marketing idea, but it almost accidentally communicated a real fact – that all malts are different in a way that is familiar to wine drinkers, who are used to the idea of differences within and between regions.

This idea of regional difference has also been justified by the existence of a division between 'Highland' and 'Lowland' regions, even though this was first introduced for tax reasons in 1781. A natural identification with region also occurred among blenders of different styles of spirit, who thought in terms of malts from 'Islay', 'Campbeltown' and 'Speyside' (originally 'Glenlivet').

There is no way of pinning down the difference for sure and perhaps the blenders' tastes have owed more to tradition and the requirements of their blending houses when buying, as those firms were (and are) the key customers for malt whisky. Today, 'Islay style' malts are being made on Speyside and 'Highland style' on Islay. So beware of thinking that 'all Islay malts are smoky' or 'all Speysides are fruity'. Notwithstanding this, allow yourself to notice the flavour profiles that do seem to attend to a particular region.

Making malt whisky
Many of the photographs in this book relate to aspects of the production and maturation processes, so I will run through these processes, in relation to how each might influence the flavour of the mature whisky.

Raw materials
By law, malt whisky may be made only from malted barley, water and yeast. 'Scotch malt whisky' must be distilled, matured and bottled in Scotland. Barley, one of the first cereal grains to be cultivated, has been grown in Scotland since Neolithic times. New strains or 'varieties' are continually being developed with a view to increasing yield (the amount of alcohol per tonne of grain) and ease of processing. The

general view of the whisky industry is that the barley variety does not have much influence on the flavour of the spirit, but some dispute this.

It used to be thought that the nature of the water used for mashing (the 'process water') was crucial; that it was the water which differentiated one make from another. The general view among Scottish distillers today is that the mineral content and pH value of the water make little difference to the flavour of the mature spirit, although, again, some distillers beg to differ.

There is a similar debate about yeast. Traditionally, a mix of brewers' and distillers' yeasts were used and it was believed that brewers' yeast contributed fruity flavours. Today, brewers' yeast has been abandoned without, it is said, affecting flavour. This surprises American and Japanese distillers, for whom the yeast strain is considered fundamental.

Malting
Malting is the process by which cell walls in the barleycorns are broken down so that the starches contained in the cells may be converted into sugars. The sugars, in turn, will be converted into alcohol during fermentation. In nature, this process occurs when the seeds sense that it is time to germinate: the starch is present in the seed, ready to feed the young plant until it has put down roots and sprouted. The malting process imitates this – in a way, it tricks the seeds into thinking that spring has arrived and it is time to burst into life and start growing.

The first stage of malting is to steep the grains in water, three times, over the course of two days, allowing air rests in between. This process increases the moisture level in the grains.

The next stage is to germinate the grains. In days gone by this was done by spreading the seeds on a concrete floor; today, germination is achieved mechanically, by placing the seeds in large drums. After around five days, the cell walls will have broken down and the grains are termed 'fully modified'.

At this stage it is important to stop the germination before the young plant consumes the precious starch. This is done by casting the grains – now called 'green malt' – into a kiln and blowing hot air through the bed for up to 30 hours.

If the distiller wants a smoky whisky, fragrant peat must be burned during the early hours of kilning. Peat is made up of long-compressed grasses, mosses and other vegetation, which has been dug from damp moorland and dried. Drying over peat has a big impact upon the flavour of the spirit and the mature whisky.

Milling

After having been rested for a spell, the dried malt is ground into 'grist' by putting it through a mill. The grist mill has two rollers: one to crack the husk, the other to grind the malt. The rollers are carefully set to produce 70 per cent grist, 20 per cent husk and 10 per cent flour. This division is essential for the next stage to work efficiently, but it has no influence upon flavour.

Mashing

The grist is now mixed with hot water in a large stainless steel or cast-iron vessel called a 'mash tun' and during this process the starch is converted into sugar by the action of enzymes. The sugar dissolves in the water and the resulting liquid is drawn off through the perforated base of the tun. The drained-off liquid is called 'wort'; it is a sweet, non-alcoholic fluid that will later become whisky. The quantity and quality of wort dictates the amount of alcohol which will be won at the end of the day. Its clarity or cloudiness also affects flavour, as cloudy worts tend to make a malty, cereal-like spirit.

Fermenting

The wort is cooled and pumped into fermenting vessels, called 'washbacks' made from larch, Douglas fir or stainless steel. Here yeast is added and after an initial quiet spell it gets to work converting the sugars into alcohol and carbon dioxide, in approximately equal amounts, over the following 48 hours. In many distilleries, the liquid (now called 'wash') is ready to be distilled, but those who want to develop more complex and delicate, fruity and floral flavours leave the wash to undergo a further bacterial fermentation for the next 12 hours at least.

Distilling

Distillation is done in copper pot stills. The spirit is always distilled twice and occasionally three times, to achieve the strength and purity required. This invariably takes place in separate stills. It is a batch process: the stills are charged, distilled off, cleaned, rested and then recharged.

The first still, called the 'wash still', is charged with beery wash at around 8% ABV ('alcohol by volume'), brought to the boil, then simmered. Since alcohol boils at a lower temperature than water, it is possible to separate the two, and this is what happens. By the end of the run, about one-third of the wash will have been saved as 'low wines' (now at around 21% vol). The low wines pass to a tank, where they are mixed with some of the fractions (the early and late runnings from a previous distillation), raising their strength to around 28% vol. This mixture fills the second or 'low wines'

still, which is brought to a simmer. The first runnings of alcohol (called 'heads' or 'foreshots') are of high strength, but they are impure and pungent. They are set aside to be redistilled for the next set of low wines.

When the spirit is deemed by the operator to be pure, which may take anything from 10 to 40 minutes, the distiller directs the liquid to the spirit receiver. This is the 'heart of the run', which will become whisky. The distiller continues to operate the still until the later runnings, called 'tails' or 'feints', begin to emerge. Like the foreshots, these have an unpleasant flavour. At this point, the distiller stops saving spirit and directs the tails to join the foreshots, so both can be redistilled. The length of time the operator saves spirit – the breadth of the 'cut' – has a profound effect on the flavour of the whisky.

Maturing

By law, the spirit must be matured in oak casks for a minimum of three years before it may be named 'whisky'. It was discovered long ago that oak was the perfect wood in which to mature whisky, wine and other spirits, on account of its strength, malleability, porosity and intricate chemistry. Two kinds of oakwood are used: American white oak and European oak. Each variety contributes different flavours and colours to the maturing spirit. All except a tiny proportion are 'secondhand': they will have been seasoned with either bourbon or sherry to draw out some of their over-oaky flavours.

Casks come in different sizes. The most common are American standard barrels, at 200 litres. In Scotland, these are often remade into hogsheads, which hold 250 litres. Butts and puncheons, which can each hold 500 litres are also used and these are usually made from European oak.

Smaller casks tend to mature their contents more rapidly than larger ones, but the key factor is how often the cask has been used; that is to say, whether it is 'first fill' or 'refill'. Cask activity declines over usage and time, so that after about three fills the cask is deemed to be 'exhausted' and it is either discarded or rejuvenated for reuse by being scraped down to fresh wood, refired and reseasoned.

The cask in which whisky matures is infinitely more than just a container: there is an old saying in Scotland that 'the wood makes the whisky'. It was once suggested that we might imagine the cask to be a chrysalis and the spirit to be a caterpillar which emerges after its long sleep as a butterfly.

Lastly, the atmosphere and microclimate of the maturation warehouse may influence the flavour of the mature whisky. Traditional 'dunnage' warehouses in Scotland are low and damp and the casks are mounted three-high. In modern warehouses casks are 'racked' seven or eight high, in warm, dry air.

So what makes the difference? Dr Douglas Murray, a chemist at Diageo, perhaps captures it best when he says, 'Of course you can capture the place in the whisky – indeed, you can't condense the spirit without capturing some of the essence of the location... We'll never know how it happens. And we don't want to.'

Charlie

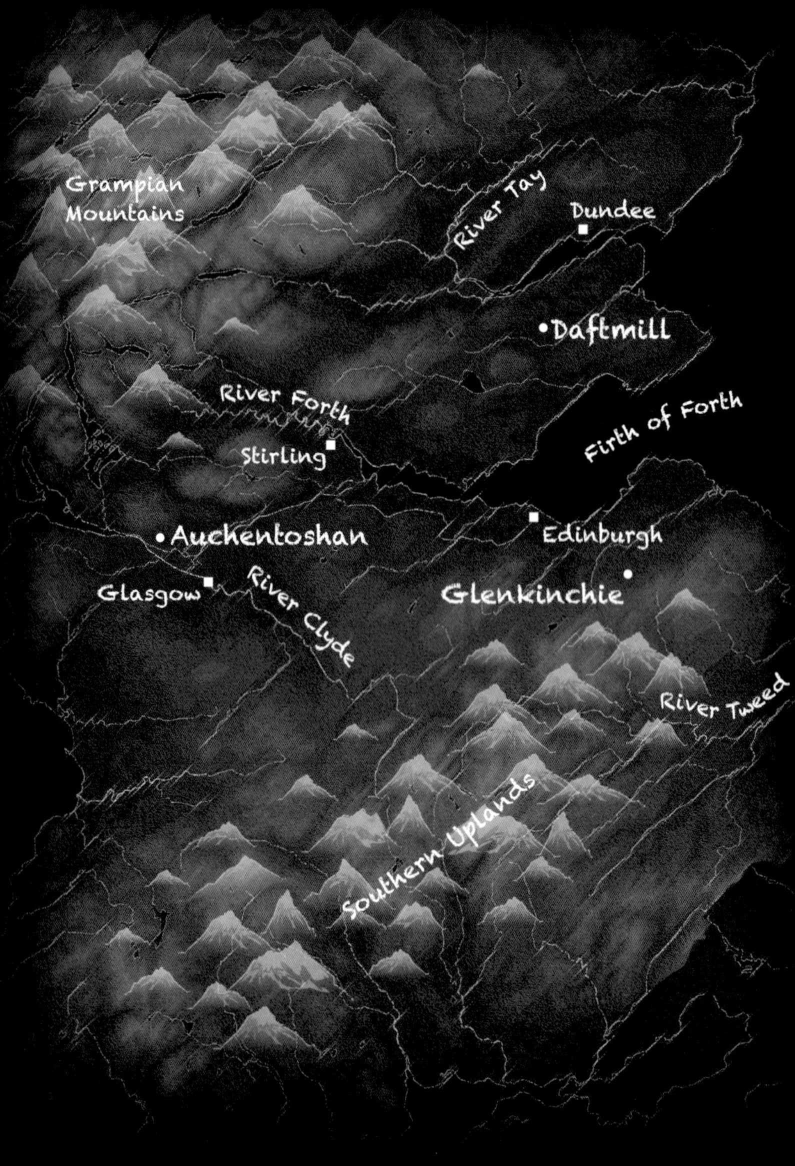

Grampian Mountains
River Tay
Dundee
Daftmill
River Forth
Firth of Forth
Stirling
Auchentoshan
Edinburgh
Glasgow
River Clyde
Glenkinchie
River Tweed
Southern Uplands

In terms of daily life, the inhabitants of the Lowlands viewed the mountain ramparts that defined the boundary with some trepidation. The Highlanders were a different tribe, who viewed the Lowlands as fair game for pillage, not least because they had a greater population and larger trading markets.

The Lowland counties below and to the east of the Highland Line (Perthshire, Angus and Aberdeenshire) were also more fertile than the Highlands and lent themselves to arable farming. During the 18th and early 19th centuries improvements were made in land fertilization and drainage, crop husbandry and harvesting, which made it possible to grow more cereals. So it is not surprising that Lowland distilling became industrialized long before it did in the Highlands.

Larger stills came into play due to excise regulations. At the same time, the Lowland farms produced many types of cereal, so distilleries used mixed mashes of grains, rather than simply malted barley. However, while many pot-still distilleries in the Lowlands produced grain whisky, those that made malt distilled a distinctive spirit, with a much lighter and drier character than that from the Highlands.

'THE CORNER OF THE FIELD'

In the 1830s, the distillery's name was changed from Bulloch's original name of 'Duntocher' to 'Auchentoshan' (pronounced 'Ock-un-tosh-un'), which translates as 'the corner of the field'. There are not many fields around the distillery today, as it stands in Clydebank, part of the City of Glasgow, but the site is surrounded by trees.

AUCHENTOSHAN

Fresh, floral and zesty

By Dalmuir, Clyebank, G81 4SJ
www.auchentoshan.com

Auchentoshan Distillery was built in 1823 on the Auchentoshan Estate, Clydebank, around 20 minutes from the centre of Glasgow. It lies in the shadow of the Old Kilpatrick Hills, overlooking the legendary River Clyde, which provided Glasgow with a route to the Americas during the Industrial Revolution. The original distillery was built by a corn merchant named John Bulloch, and the early years were a struggle: both John and his son went bankrupt, and in 1834 the distillery was sold to Alexander Filshie, a local farmer. Filshie's family had lived in the neighbourhood since the 1600s, and they were to own Auchentoshan for 44 years before having to sell in 1877 following a disastrous harvest. In 1903 the distillery passed to the Glasgow firm of John & George MacLachlan, brewers and distillers.

By the late 1800s the landscape around the distillery had changed beyond recognition. Glasgow was said to be the second-most important city in the British Empire, and it was famous for its heavy engineering – particularly railway engines and ships.

The River Clyde was the highway to the world and its banks were crowded with wharfs and docks. The town of Clydebank grew up around Auchentoshan, following the establishment of a Singer Sewing Machine factory and two major shipyards. However, in the course of two nights in March 1941, Clydebank was destroyed by German bombers, who were targeting the shipyards. More than 1,000 people were killed and only seven properties remained unharmed. Miraculously, the distillery was one of them, although three warehouses and over one million litres of whisky were lost. A bomb crater behind the distillery now forms the pond for cooling water.

The post-war years saw further changes in ownership, but also a rise in the availability and popularity of Auchentoshan single malt. In 1984 the distillery was bought by the whisky blenders Stanley P Morrison, who later became Morrison Bowmore Distillers Ltd. In 1994 the firm was sold to Suntory, a Japanese group that has been distilling whisky since 1924.

15

THE MASH TUN

The distillery has a modern stainless steel, semi-Lauter mash tun, with a smart copper canopy. In this vessel the grist (ground malt) is mixed with hot water to produce the sweet liquid known as wort. Once cooled in a heat exchanger, the wort is pumped into the washbacks, or fermenting vessels, where yeast is added to produce a beery liquid known as wash, which will be distilled.

TRIPLE DISTILLATION ▶

In days gone by, many distilleries in the Scottish Lowlands employed three stills, rather than the usual two, to produce an extra-refined spirit by triple distillation. Today, Auchentoshan is the only distillery to carry on this tradition. It is a complex process, but the result is a lighter, purer, smoother and more delicate spirit, with fruity and floral flavours, developed and filled out during maturation.

A MIX OF CASKS ▶

Each expression of Auchentoshan single malt (i.e. each different bottling) has its own mix of casks: first-fill and refill ex-bourbon barrels and ex-sherry butts (both oloroso and Pedro Ximénez); virgin oak; and refill hogsheads. Although they are all made of oak, each imparts different flavours to its contents, according to whether they are made from American or Spanish oak and whether they have been seasoned with bourbon or sherry.

A RANGE OF EXPRESSIONS ▶

The core range of expressions is at 12, 18 and 21 years: 'Classic', 'Three Wood' and 'Vallinch'. There are also annual limited edition bottlings at 30, 40 and 50 years old.

PRESERVING TRADITION
Glenkinchie has an interesting museum that
includes this old riveted pot still and a 1:6 scale
model of a whisky distillery built in 1924 for the
British Empire Exhibition at Wembley, London.

GLENKINCHIE

Fresh, grassy and lemony

Pencaitland, Tranent EH34 5ET
www.discovering-distilleries.com

Glenkinchie Distillery stands in a wooded glen on the edge of the village of Pencaitland, in East Lothian, 15 miles from Edinburgh. East Lothian's beauty is legendary; the poet Robert Burns described it as 'the most glorious corn country I have ever seen.' East Lothian was also the cradle of the agricultural revolution in Scotland. John Cockburn of Ormiston, the 'father of Scottish husbandry' and founder of the Society of Improvers of Knowledge of Agriculture in 1723, owned land here. The revolution in farming that he helped to bring about introduced exotic vegetables such as the potato, cabbage and turnip, while improved farming methods increased the amount of cereals that could be produced. Breweries and distilleries were among the Society's recommendations for taking up the surplus.

Brothers John and George Rate founded Glenkinchie in 1837, after they had established a former small distillery at Milton on the Ormiston estate 12 years earlier. They went bankrupt in 1852 and the next owner of the property used it as a sawmill. However, by 1880 the market for blended Scotch whisky was growing rapidly and the site attracted attention. Before long, a consortium of brewers and whisky merchants resumed distillation at Glenkinchie, and in 1890 they rebuilt the whole site in old red brick, which is unusual for Scotland; indeed I cannot think of any other malt distillery which uses this material so extensively.

Glenkinchie was one of five Lowland distilleries that joined together to create Scottish Malt Distillers (SMD) in 1914. This became the production division of the mighty Distillers Company Ltd (DCL) in the 1920s. At around the same time, Glenkinchie was licensed to John Haig & Company and so became a key filling for Haig White Label, a bestselling blend in the 1960s. The distillery's current owners, Diageo, inherited the distillery when it took over DCL in 1997.

19

▲ VICTORIAN BUILDINGS

The stone building shown to the left in this image is one of the few remaining parts of the pre-1890 distillery. The brick building on the right is part of the old maltings.

◀ SCOTLAND'S LARGEST STILLS

Glenkinchie's two copper pot stills are the largest in Scotland. Together, they produce around 1.5 million litres of whisky each year. The spirit is cooled in a single cast-iron worm tub, rather than a modern condenser, to give the whisky a deeper flavour.

REFILL HOGSHEADS ▶

The casks used to mature Glenkinchie spirit are almost entirely 'refill hogsheads'. In other words, they have been used at least once before for maturing Scotch whisky and they have a capacity of around 250 litres. The origin of the word 'hogshead' is obscure. The best derivation I have heard of comes from the cider trade, where it was customary in days gone by to add a lump of pig meat – even a pig/hog's head – to the barrel to add flavour. Most Glenkinchie spirit is matured off-site, but the casks used for single malt bottlings are retained, or returned for maturation in the distillery's traditional warehouses.

THE OLD MILL
The inspiration for the distillery was
this elegant old mill building, part
of which dates from the late 17th
century. The building forms one side
of the square site and is used as a
malt store; the pagoda roof is a recent
addition and purely decorative.

DAFTMILL

Robust and oily, with fennel

Cupar, Fife KY15 5RF
www.daftmill.com

Daftmill Farm lies a couple of miles from the town of Cupar in Fife, in an area which, like East Lothian, is rich arable land. The farm has been owned by the Cuthbert family for six generations, and has long grown malting barley for the whisky industry. The current owners, Ian and Francis Cuthbert, discovered substantial deposits of gravel on the farm a few years ago and they established a quarry. This was highly lucrative, but rather than invest the income – which they saw as their 'pension fund' – they decided to restore an old mill building on the farm and convert it into a distillery. The licence was granted in 2005.

The mill building itself dates from the late 17th century, with additions in the 18th and early 19th; a date stone in the gable is inscribed 1809. The building forms one side of an open square and is now used as a malt store; opposite the mill is a stone barn which has been converted into a traditional dunnage warehouse. The distillery sits at right angles to these buildings. With a capacity of 60,000 litres of pure alcohol per year, this is one of the smallest distilleries in Scotland.

The whole ensemble is neat and compact – indeed I would rank Daftmill as among the most attractive of all malt distilleries. The first whisky was produced in December 2005, using water from Daftmill's natural spring. So far the whisky has not been bottled for sale and the brothers are in no hurry. Francis Cuthbert simply says, 'We'll bottle when we think it's ready.'

THE STILL HOUSE
Daftmill's compact still house holds two small stills: a wash-still and a spirit still. The wash-still is charged with 2,500 litres of liquid, while the spirit still holds 1,500 litres. To put this in context, the largest wash-still in Scotland (*see* Glenkinchie, *pp. 18–21*) is 20,000 litres.

▲ THE LOMOND HILLS

Also known as 'The Paps of Fife', the Lomond Hills are conspicuous for miles around. In their shadow is the ancient village of Falkland, where stands Falkland Palace, once a royal hunting lodge. Daftmill Distillery is situated on the fertile low ground below, which is known as the Howe o'Fife. This was once a royal forest, preserved for hunting deer, and it now provides Daftmill with its barley.

THE WATER TOWER ▶

The farm's water tower is a local landmark and provides the distillery with water. It is thought to have been built by a Dutch engineer who was in the area to help build the Tay Rail Bridge. Water used to be pumped from an artesian well to the large water tank at the top; these days an electrical pump does all the hard work.

25

Mull

Firth of Lorn

Colonsay

Jura

Bunnahabhain

Caol Ila

Islay

Kilchoman

Bruichladdich

Bowmore

Laphroaig

Ardbeg

Lagavulin

ISLAY

Islay is the most southerly of the Western Isles, only around 11 miles from the north coast of Ireland, and it is possible, even likely, that the island was the cradle of whisky distilling in Scotland. It is the most fertile of the Western Isles, although today barley is imported. Fuel is plentiful, in the form of peat and there is no shortage of pure water from the lochs and rivers. It is believed that whisky may have been made on the island as far back as the 14th century and its relative remoteness encouraged widespread smuggling. A tax was levied on whisky in 1644, but the island was considered to be so full of 'barbarians' that no excise man (or 'gauger') was brave enough to set foot on Islay until 1797.

The malt whisky made on Islay is famously smoky. Three distilleries have their own floor maltings (Laphroaig, Kilchoman and Bowmore) and can produce at least part of their requirement; the rest is made at Port Ellen Maltings, where it is peated to precisely specified levels. The process and the island seem not to have changed much since Alfred Barnard's visit to Islay in 1885, when the famous whisky historian wrote, 'The air was crisp and the first few hours of the long drive chilly, but the morning sun soon filled our hearts with gladness, and we were enabled once again to enjoy the delightful scenery through which we passed.'

A COASTAL DISTILLERY

Ardbeg Distillery lies on the rocky shoreline near Port Ellen and has
its own pier. The small cargo ships known as 'puffers' were frequent
visitors here in the early 20th century, delivering empty casks and
yeast, and picking up whisky and bags of draff for animal feed.

ARDBEG

Sweet and smoky

Argyll, Port Ellen, Isle of Islay, PA42 7EA
www.ardbeg.com

Islay may be the original home of Scottish whisky distilling, where it began under the medieval Lords of the Isles, who patronized musicians and poets, jewellery and weapon-makers, stone carvers and physicians. At the time, distillation was a branch of medicine, so fell under this patronage. The first written reference to distilling malted barley in Scotland is found in a royal accounts book of 1494; that year the king, James IV, had been campaigning on Islay against the Lord of the Isles, and it is possible that he first encountered distilled spirits, known as *aqua vitae* or 'the water of life' on Islay. The Gaelic for *aqua vitae* is *uisge beatha,* from which the word 'whisky' derives.

The hereditary physicians to both the Lordship and the Scottish Crown came from a family named MacBeatha, anglicized to 'Beaton'. They arrived in Scotland in 1300, in the marriage train of an Irish princess who was to wed Angus Og MacDonald, Lord of the South Isles. At the time of their arrival, the MacBeathas were known to be 'wise physicians' and it is likely that they brought the secrets of distilling for medical purposes with them from Ireland.

'Private' distilling, for personal or community use and not for sale, was legal until 1781. After it was banned, it went underground and by the late 18th century it was endemic throughout Scotland – not least on Islay. By the 18th century most of Islay was owned by members of Clan Campbell and it was these 'improving lairds' who encouraged their tenants to establish licensed commercial whisky distilleries. Walter Frederick Campbell, laird of Kildalton Parish on the rocky south coast of the island (home to Ardbeg, Lagavulin and Laphroaig distilleries), encouraged John MacDougall to take out a licence.

Ardbeg Distillery was founded in 1815. Like all the other distilleries on the island, except the recently established Kilchoman (*see pp. 44–7*), it was situated on the coast, so that imports of coal, barley and casks and exports of whisky, could take place by sea. This was an important factor when roads were primitive and a stone pier was built to facilitate the sea trade.

By 1835 the distillery was making around 2,300 litres of spirit a week and was the largest on the island. By this time the tenant was John MacDougall's son, Alexander, a 'stout and loyal clansman' who, when he learned that a kinsman had been found guilty of some misdemeanour, immediately paid the fine, saying that it was impossible that a MacDougall could do any wrong! But the boom years were not to last: by the late 1850s, Alexander MacDougall's sisters, who now held the licence, were obliged to sell to their partner and financial backer, Thomas Grey Buchanan.

Luckily for Buchanan and his successor, the fortunes of the whisky industry were on the upturn by the 1870s and Islay was especially popular with the whisky blenders. By 1900, the village that had grown up around the distillery housed the families of 40 workers and the school had more than 100 pupils.

However, by the 1920s, sales were in decline. They continued to suffer during the war years, before improving again during the 1960s. By the mid-1970s demand outstripped supply, but then the distillery's key customers cut their orders substantially. In 1976 Hiram Walker acquired control of the distillery.

Ardbeg's fortunes improved dramatically when the distillery was bought by Glenmorangie in 1997. By then the site had become dilapidated and the new owners spent £1.4 million on its restoration. They also invested heavily in building the Ardbeg brand as a single malt: today it enjoys cult status, supported by over 60,000 fans in the 'Ardbeg Committee'.

KILDALTON CROSS
The magnificent Kildalton Cross, which stands close to Ardbeg distillery, is a masterpiece of 8th-century religious art. It is among the finest and most important Celtic High Crosses in Scotland. Reaching 2.65 metres in height, it has a span of 1.32 metres and stands in the same place upon which it was erected over 1,200 years ago.

BLACK CATTLE

Shaggy Highland longhorn cows were predominantly black until Queen Victoria began to select and breed the ginger-coloured strains that are known today as 'Highland cows'. The Highland economy was based upon such cattle. In the early 19th century, Aberdeen Angus cattle, such as those seen here, were developed from the Highland breed – they are hornless and have shorter coats.

BOWMORE

Smoky and floral

School Street, Bowmore, Isle Of Islay PA43 7JS
www.bowmore.com

Bowmore is the oldest licensed distillery on Islay and one of the oldest in Scotland – if not *the* oldest. The date ascribed to its foundation by its owners is 1779, but I believe it may have been established a decade earlier, when the model village of Bowmore was built by Daniel Campbell of Shawfield. Campbell's father, another Daniel, was MP for the city of Glasgow. In 1725 he voted in favour of a malt tax, as a result of which the mob looted his house and broke all his windows. The government of the day paid him £9,000 in compensation and with this he bought the island of Islay.

Campbell brought in a man named David Simson from the neighbouring village of Bridgend to build the distillery. In time, Campbell was succeeded by a relative, Hector Simson, who later sold to James and William Mutter, Glasgow merchants of German extraction. They expanded the distillery and developed the whisky's reputation. In 1841, the new laird, Walter Frederick Campbell, received an order from Windsor Castle to supply 'a cask of your best Islay Mountain Dew' for the Royal Household; cask size and price were of no concern, but it should be 'the very best that can be had.' The order was renewed two years later.

The Mutter brothers owned a steamship to carry casks up to Glasgow, where they were stored under the arches of Glasgow Central Station (now a large nightclub). Unusually for the time, Bowmore was sold as a single malt in the 1890s as well as going into blended Scotch. A bottle engraved 'W & J Mutter 1890' was sold in 2001 for the unusually high sum of £13,000. Just six years later, another bottle, allegedly from 1851, fetched £25,000.

In 1963 the Bowmore distillery was bought by a Glasgow whisky broker by the name of Stanley P Morrison; Suntory took a 34 per cent share of the company in 1989 and became outright owners in 1994, continuing today.

Bowmore is one of only nine distilleries to have its own maltings. They produce 30 per cent of its requirement, while the rest comes from an independent maltster on the mainland. Local peat is burned in the malt kiln and contributes to the unique style of the spirit.

◄ THE STILL HOUSE

Bowmore has two pairs of stills; unusually – if not uniquely – all four are fitted with sight-glasses. These small windows into to the neck of the still are usually fitted only to wash stills, so the still-man can tell how far the boiling wash has risen up the neck and turn down the heat before it flows over into the swan neck.

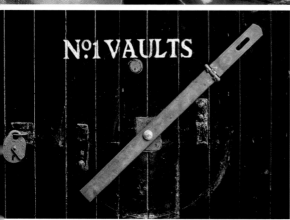

◄ BOWMORE VAULTS

The three-storey 'No. 1 Warehouse', of which the ground floor is known as 'the vaults', dates from the distillery's foundation. The vaults themselves are below sea level; the thick walls are salt-encrusted in places and ooze damp. The atmosphere is cool and briny and it is likely that this influences the flavour of the whisky matured under these conditions.

◄ BOWMORE DISTILLERY

All the coastal distilleries on Islay – in other words, all but Kilchoman – have their names painted boldly on the side of their sea-facing warehouses. This is more than just advertising: in the past it helped ships navigating through fog know where they were in relation to the coast.

NON-CONFORMIST DISTILLERS

Bruichladdich is vocally non-conformist and independent. It describes itself as 'The Outsider' and its Gaelic motto, *Clachan a Choin*, means 'the dog's bollocks'. To those who object to their outspoken stand, they quote film producer Orson Welles: 'No one who takes on anything big and tough can afford to be modest'. The striking aquamarine livery adopted by the company – inspired by the (sometimes!) brilliant blue water of Loch Indaal – is typical of their mould-breaking brand positioning.

BRUICHLADDICH

Light, grassy and malty

Isle of Islay, PA49 7UN
www.bruichladdich.com

Bruichladdich (pronounced 'Brewick-laddie') was purpose-built in 1881 using concrete, a material that had only recently been rediscovered (it had been widely used by the Romans and even earlier by the Mycenaeans of Bronze Age Greece). The distillery was designed by a young engineer named Robert Harvey, using knowledge gained from his family's century-long experience of distilling in Glasgow. The Harvey family owned Glasgow's Yoker and Dundas Hill distilleries, and Robert was joined in the new venture on Islay by his brothers John, who provided the whisky-making expertise, and William, a businessman.

Built to make the most of gravitation, the distillery was situated on a hill, so the brewing tanks sat above a downward run of mash tuns, cooker, refrigerator and tun room. This kept pumping – then powered by steam – to a minimum. William's son Rudd claimed that his uncle Robert also invented a double-ended key device for preventing a vacuum forming in the system, which went on to become widely used in other Scottish stills. Sadly, however, the three lads had more enthusiasm than business sense and the young firm floundered. It continued to have a mixed history until 2000, when it was bought by a private concern led by Mark Reynier, a London wine merchant, with the support of local investors, for £6.5 million.

Reynier's family were the founders of wine merchants La Reserve, in Soho, London, and later the independent and well-respected whisky bottler, Murray McDavid. With a deep knowledge of wine, Mark Reynier pioneered a wine-finishing programme for the whisky at Bruichladdich, which he named 'additional cask evolution' (ACE-ing). This involves re-racking mature whisky for varying lengths of time in wine barrels.

35

Among the original investors was James McEwan, a local man who had started at Bowmore Distillery (*see pp.32–3*) as an apprentice cooper in 1963. He ran the warehouses there until 1977, when he moved to Glasgow and spent the next seven years as a blender at Morrison Bowmore's head office. McEwan returned to Bowmore as manager in 1984, just as malt whisky was beginning to take off, and was soon spending much of his time travelling the world, tirelessly promoting Bowmore, Islay and Scotland. McEwan was persuaded to join Bruichladdich as production director when Murray McDavid & Co took over.

The firm took its inspiration from the spirit of innovation that had created the distillery in the first place, and released a number of special and commemorative bottlings. These have included Yellow Submarine, to mark the discovery of a bright yellow, unmanned sub-sea vessel by a local fisherman (for a long time the Admiralty denied all knowledge of it!); Octomore, the most heavily peated whisky in the world; Usquebaugh-baul, which translates as 'Perilous whisky' (it is quadruple-distilled and filled into cask at 88% vol); and The Laddie Ten (Bruichladdich's colloquial name). This last became the standard bottling. When I asked Mark Reynier why they released so many expressions, which were confusing consumers, frustrating retailers and infuriating collectors (who couldn't keep up), he simply replied: 'Because we can. And we're having fun.'

Reynier left the distillery in 2012,

but Bruichladdich's credo remains the same: 'We believe that Islay whisky should be the ultimate expression of the island itself; an authenticity derived from where it is distilled and where it is matured...from the philosophies of those who distil it. A sense of place, of terroir that speaks of the land, the water, the barley and the human soul that gave it life.' The distillery uses the term 'terroir' in the full knowledge of its denigration by some firms, for whom, they say, it is 'commercially inconvenient.' For Bruichladdich however, it represents the many, many centuries of profound farming experience behind the land that now gives rise to their whisky. It is perhaps with the guiding notion of terroir that the distillery has released a number of limited bottlings of different barley varieties, coming from different farms around Islay.

The distillery today is very traditional in style, and still operates with the ancient cast-iron, rake-and-plough mash tun that dates from 1881, six Oregon-pine washbacks and two pairs of stills. They also have a separate 'Lomond' still (affectionately known as 'ugly Betty'), which came from the Inverleven Distillery and in which they make the excellent Botanist Gin. This uses 22 local 'botanicals', or herbs, foraged from around the hills, peat bogs and shoreline of Islay. Today, Bruichladdich is one of only three distilleries to bottle all its whisky on site, reducing to bottling strength (usually 50% vol) with specially collected spring water (*see facing page*) from a farm nearby.

◄ **WHISKY LEGEND**
When Jim McEwan was persuaded to transfer to the independently owned Bruichladdich Distillery as Director of Production in 2000, he was already a legend in the whisky trade in which he had worked for nearly 40 years. His decision and hard work on behalf of his new company, in which he held shares, paid off when it was sold in 2013 to Rémy Cointreau. He remains as Master Distiller.

PURE SPRING WATER ▼
The distillery's cooling water comes from the Bruichladdich Burn and its process water comes from Loch an Torran, two miles above the distillery, which provides soft and peaty water. Unusually, the distillery also uses a third water source: a crystal-clear spring on Octomore Farm, behind the village of Port Charlotte. James Brown, the farmer who owns the land, collects this precious water and it is used for reducing the strength of the whisky when it is bottled at the distillery, typically to 50% vol.

THE SCIENCE OF MATURATION ▼
Bruichladdich's whisky is matured in 12 large racked warehouses. In 2012, Professor Otto Hermelin of Stockholm began research into the maturation process by monitoring how changes in temperature and humidity affect the maturation in four of Islay's distilleries (Bruichladdich, Kilchoman, Bunnahabhain and Ardbeg). He tests casks filled at the same time from the same batch of newly made spirit, but stored at different heights in the warehouses. The study is expected to last ten years.

BUNNAHABHAIN FRONTAGE

Like all the coastal distilleries on Islay, Bunnahabhain's
name is painted large against a white background
on its sea-facing walls. However, unlike many of
them, Bunnahabhain built a pier early on to allow for
the landing of barley, coal and empty casks, and the
shipment of full casks to the mainland. Other distilleries
used 'puffers', small coastal cargo vessels with flat
bottoms, which could be run up onto the beach.

BUNNAHABHAIN

Fruity, lightly maritime, hint of smoke

Port Askaig, Isle of Islay, PA46 7RP
www.bunnahabhain.com

Bunnahabhain's situation on the north coast of Islay is among the most remote of any distillery in Scotland. It overlooks the Sound of Islay – a narrow strait between Islay and Jura – and has a fine view of the neighbouring island. The distillery founder was William Robertson, senior partner in the Glasgow firm of whisky brokers Robertson & Baxter (R&B), in conjunction with the Greenlees Brothers, who owned Hazelburn Distillery in Campbeltown and the Lorne, Old Parr and Claymore blends.

The improbable site was chosen on account of R&B's close relationship with another Glasgow firm of blenders, Bulloch Lade & Company, who owned Caol Ila Distillery further down the Sound of Islay at Port Askaig and had recently extended and improved it. The copious waters of Loch Staoinsha, sitting in hills above the site, also affected the choice, because they could be used to cool the condensers (the distillery's process water comes from springs in the Margadale Hills).

Work began on the site in 1881 and the distillery was commissioned in January 1883, at the dawn of the 'whisky boom', a period of unprecedented growth in which blended Scotch rapidly replaced brandy as the most fashionable drink in England and the British Empire. Although R&B did not own any brands of blended Scotch at the time, the spirit to be made at Bunnahabhain was to be used for blending. As such, it was unpeated, since the fashion then was for lighter blends rather than the robust and smoky whiskies that preceded them.

The founding company was named Islay Distillers; this was changed to Highland Distilleries in 1887, when R&B acquired Glenrothes Distillery on Speyside (*see pp. 204–7*). In the 1920s, R&B were commissioned by Berry Bros & Rudd, the long-established wine and spirits merchant in London, to blend Cutty Sark – a brand in which they held a 50 per cent share – and Bunnahabhain became a key 'filling whisky'. In 1971, Highland acquired The Famous Grouse, also blended by R&B.

Because of its popularity with blenders, Bunnahabhain was not made available as a single malt until the late 1970s. It is often described as 'Islay's mildest malt', although it is full of character, with a rich texture and a sweet, very slightly smoky taste.

THE SOUND OF ISLAY
This is the view from the coast near Bunnahabhain, across the perilously tidal Sound of Islay to the Paps of Jura. The site is remote and exposed, and building here was not without its difficulties – during the first winter of building, two large boilers, waiting to be fitted, were blown off the beach.

A 'NOBLE GATEWAY' ▶

Whisky historian Alfred Barnard visited Bunnahabhain in 1886 and wrote, 'A fine pile of buildings in the form of a square and quite enclosed. Entering by the noble gateway one forms an immediate sense of the compactness and symmetrical construction of the work.' Along with the distillery, the buildings comprised houses, a school and a village hall for the workforce. A pier was built out into the fast-flowing Sound and a mile-long road was constructed up the steep cliff behind the distillery to join the track to Port Askaig.

MEN AT WORK ▶

During the 1960s Bunnahabhain was 'modernized'; a second pair of stills was installed and all four were converted to indirect firing by steam coils and pans within the stills themselves. This allowed heat to be easily controlled by turning a stopcock. Previously, when the stills were direct-fired from below by coal, the hot embers needed to be physically raked out to reduce heat, which was a hot and dirty job.

COLLECTING THE SPENT GRAINS ▶

The distillery is unusual in retaining its traditional mash tun – a large, cast-iron vessel equipped with a 'rake-and-plough' gear to stir the mash. At the end of a mashing, the mash tun is emptied of the residues of distilling, including husks and spent grains. The residue is known as 'draff' and it has a second life as a highly nutritious cattle feed.

41

▲ STENCILLING
THE CASKS
Until recently, the heads of
the casks in which the spirit
matures were stencilled with the
cask number and the names of
the distillery and cask owner.
The casks were supplied by
the blending house that had
ordered the whisky and each
house painted the cask heads
in their own distinctive colour –
which made for a very colourful
warehouse! Sadly, this is no
longer the case and the casks are
identified merely by bar codes.

◄ A STILL WITH A VIEW
The still house at Caol Ila has,
arguably, the finest view of any
malt distillery, looking across the
Sound of Islay to the Paps of Jura.
The stills themselves are plain
or 'onion' shaped, allowing for
good contact between the alcohol
vapour and the copper, which
makes a lighter style of spirit.

CAOL ILA

Sweet, with fragrant smoke and antiseptic cream

Port Askaig, Isle of Islay, PA46 7RL
www.discovering-distilleries.com

The distillery takes its name from the long stretch of water it overlooks: the Sound of Islay, known as *Caol Ila* in Gaelic. This furiously tidal passage sits between Islay and Jura, and the distillery was built by one Hector Henderson on a bay near the ferry terminal at Port Askaig. Henderson had been a partner in the firm that owned Littlemill Distillery at Bowling on the River Clyde. The site had two main attractions: easy access to the seaways, and the fast-running stream from Loch nam Ban (the 'fair' or 'white' loch), which could be used to turn a waterwheel for generating power. Unusually, for many years, the cooling water at Caol Ila has been augmented by sea water.

In his most lyrical vein, the great Victorian whisky writer Alfred Barnard says that 'ever and anon, the fragrant breeze from the myrtle and blooming heather is wafted' over the loch. He also describes the distillery as being 'on the very verge of the sea… in a deep recess of the mountain, mostly cut out of the solid rock.' Strangely, this is not the general impression.

The distillery was established as early as 1846, but the founder and his successor both went bankrupt. In 1863 it was taken over by the well-known Glasgow blender, Bulloch Lade & Company, who

extended it substantially in 1887 and built a fine pier, permitting access at any state of the tide. The distillery then began to supply traditional, smoky whisky to the blending trade.

In the early 1920s, Caol Ila was managed for a while by Robertson & Baxter (R&B), another well-known Glasgow blender and broker, who spent a lot of money making general improvements and reducing costs. R&B went on to become part of Edrington (owners of The Famous Grouse, and the Macallan and Highland Park Distilleries), but in the mid-1920s they too began to face difficulties, and sold Caol Ila and Bulloch Lade to the Distillers Company Ltd, with whom it remains under their present name, Diageo.

The original distillery was demolished in 1972 (apart from the three-storey warehouse which stands nearby) and replaced by a larger and more efficient building, which took the number of stills from two to six. In 2011–12 it was again expanded to increase capacity to 6.4 million litres of pure alcohol. The make was entirely used for blending until 1989, when a single malt was released by its owners in their well-loved 'Flora & Fauna' series, at 15 years old.

HOME-GROWN MALT
The fine sandy soil of Rockside Farm, where Kilchoman stands, grows top-quality barley for the distillery. Before the 1960s, every Scottish distillery had its own maltings, but today the number has dwindled to nine, of which only two (*Glen Ord, pp.108–11* and *Springbank, pp.146–51*) meet all their distillery's requirement. Kilchoman makes around 30 per cent of its own malt, taking the balance from Port Ellen maltings.

KILCHOMAN

Sweet, fruity and smoky

Rockside Farm, Bruichladdich, Isle of Islay PA49 7UT
www.kilchomandistillery.com

Kilchoman is one of the smallest distilleries in Scotland, one of the most recently opened (I officiated, back in 2005) and currently the most westerly, lying within Rockside Farm, near Machir Bay. It is the only landlocked distillery on Islay and now the only distillery in Scotland that does everything on site, from growing the barley to bottling the whisky. It even uses the spent draff from the distilling process as food for its cattle. In this sense, it is a true 'farm distillery', echoing the practices of 19th-century distilleries and its slogan is: 'taking whisky back to its roots.'

The current owner of Kilchoman, Anthony Wills, ran an independent single-malt bottling company before deciding to start a new distillery on Islay. The move was possibly inspired by his marriage to Cathy Wilks, a local woman whose family has a history of creating the great and glorious – her grandfather and great-uncle designed and manufactured the first Land Rover. By 2014, Cathy and Anthony's sons, Peter, James and George were also involved in running the distillery, making it a real family business. The one exception among the key team here is the legendary John MacLellan, who worked at Bunnahabhain Distillery (*see pp. 38–41*) for 20 years, rising from mash-man to general manager and in the process becoming a gifted master distiller. He joined Kilchoman as general manager in 2010.

These days, Kilchoman produces two types of whisky: 100 per cent Islay, which uses only barley grown on the island, and various commercial seasonal releases, which are made using barley grown on the mainland and kilned at the Port Ellen Maltings, some 20 miles away to the south. Everything is done by hand, which may explain the interest of the many would-be distillers who come here to learn the art during a five-day course.

SKILLED WORK

Malting in the traditional way
is labour intensive and time
consuming and it requires
considerable skill. Once the
barleycorns have been steeped,
they are spread out on a cement
floor to a depth of about 30 cm
and allowed to germinate. This
generates heat, so the grain has
to be continually turned, day and
night, with wooden shovels and
rakes to keep the temperature
even and prevent the little rootlets
becoming entangled and 'matting'.
This continues for about a week,
then the 'green malt' is transferred
to a kiln and dried. At Kilchoman
the Wills family burn peat during
the early hours of drying, to give
the whisky a smoky flavour.

OPERATING THE STILLS

Kilchoman has two stills, a plain wash-still (*above*) and a boil-ball spirit still (*right*). If the man-door on the plain still is opened to allow air to circulate, it 'revives' the copper and makes for a purer, lighter spirit. In the spirit still, the spirit run is divided into three fractions: the first runnings ('foreshots') are impure and are sent for redistillation; the middle fraction (the 'heart') is saved and put into casks; the final runnings ('feints') join the foreshots to be redistilled. The judgment of when to switch from one fraction to the next is crucial and is done manually at the spirit safe.

LAGAVULIN

Rich, fruity, fragrant smoke

Distillery Cottages, Lagavulin, Isle of Islay PA42 7DZ
www.discovering-distilleries.com

Lagavulin is a highly distinguished malt whisky, which used to be referred to as 'The Prince of Islays'. In 1887, the indefatigable 'distillery bagger' Alfred Barnard wrote: 'There are only a few of the Scotch distillers that can turn out spirit for use as single whiskies and that made at Lagavulin can claim to be one of the most prominent.'

Illicit distilling is rumoured to have started at Lagavulin in 1742 and in 1816 a local farmer named John Johnston set up the first legal distillery. By the time of Barnard's visit, the distillery was owned by J L Mackie & Co, whisky brokers and blenders in Glasgow. Three years later, the eponymous James Logan Mackie was succeeded as senior partner by his nephew Peter. Described by a contemporary as 'one-third genius, one-third megalomaniac, one-third eccentric', Peter Mackie became one of the leading characters of the whisky trade. He was known as 'Restless Peter' and countered all counsels for caution with the words: 'Nothing is impossible'. However, when Laphroaig Distillery, which stands next door to Lagavulin, dismissed J L Mackie & Co as their agents for new spirit in 1908, Peter Mackie was unable to persuade them to reverse their decision. Furious, he attempted to dam up their water supply, then decided to open a second distillery at Lagavulin that would make a spirit to compete with Laphroaig. He resolved to make it 'according to techniques believed to have been used by the pre-industrial Islay distillers'. The second distillery (and the whisky it produced) was named Malt Mill. It had two stills and three small washbacks and its malt was dried only over a peat fire. It operated for 54 years, until 1962; the building in which it was located is now a visitor centre.

There are no known (reliable) bottles of Malt Mill, but in 2012 the film director Ken Loach released an award-winning film, *The Angels' Share*, which features the auction of a cask of Malt Mill. The film (in which I had the honour of playing a 'whisky expert') won the Jury Prize at Cannes in 2012. Shortly after the film's release, a small bottle of the spirit from the very last distillation was discovered at Lagavulin Distillery.

Peter Mackie was made a baronet in 1920 and his company joined the Distillers Company Ltd (now Diageo) after his death. In 1988, they chose Lagavulin to represent the Islay style in their 'Classic Malts Selection'. The demand for Lagavulin is now so high that the whisky has to be rationed in each of its markets.

LAGAVULIN BAY

At the narrow entrance of the bay in which Lagavulin stands are the ruins of Dunyveg Castle, comprising a tower and a courtyard, with a seagate allowing access to the bay. Here the Lords of the Isles kept their galleys of war, secure behind the castle walls. The name, Dunyveg, means 'the fort of the small ships'. These vessels were highly manoeuvrable and they gave the Lords sway over all the Southern Hebrides as far as the Isle of Man.

SEASIDE DISTILLERY
Laphroaig sits beside a rocky inlet on the south coast of the island. Between the two groups of buildings – warehouse and offices to the right and maltings to the left – there is a short slipway, where coastal steamers landed coal, casks and barley and took away casks of whisky, right up until the 1970s.

LAPHROAIG

Sweet, salty and very smoky

Port Ellen, Isle of Islay PA42 7DU
www.laphroaig.com

Laphroaig proudly presents itself as 'the world's most richly flavoured Scotch whisky'. It is heavily peated – the distillery is one of the few to have its own maltings – but its smoky, medicinal, seaweedy, even tarry flavour has an unexpected sweetness to start with. Not long ago it was being advertised as 'uncompromising' and it does seem to be a malt that people either love or hate – there's no middle position!

Laphroaig stands on the shore of Loch Laphroaig on Islay's south coast. The distillery was founded in 1815 by two brothers, Donald and Alexander Johnston, who leased 1,000 acres from the Laird of Islay, initially for raising cattle. It soon became apparent that ale and whisky were more commercial options and Laphroaig quickly made a name for itself. In 1836, Donald bought out his brother and Alexander emigrated to Australia, where he lived until 1881. Donald, however, was not so lucky; only 11 years after buying out his brother, he fell into a vat of boiling ale and drowned. Ownership of the distillery was passed first to his son Dugald and thereafter down the family line. In 1921, Donald's great-grandson, Ian Hunter, became the manager and sole owner of the business. He is recognized as the man who really built the brand, although the label still pays homage to Donald, describing the owner as 'D Johnston & Company'.

Unusually, Laphroaig was sold as a single malt from the early days and by the time that Hunter took charge of the distillery, Mackie & Co of Glasgow had been acting as the malt's agents for more than 70 years. One of Hunter's first tasks on taking control was to terminate this agreement. Peter Mackie (later Sir Peter) was furious; Mackie's had, after all, established Laphroaig's reputation in the whisky trade. A powerful figure in the trade, Mackie was described as a wilful and eccentric character and his response to Hunter's dismissal was to take the firm to court. After losing the case, he tried (and failed) to block Laphroaig's water supply before finally resolving to make his own 'Laphroaig' at Lagavulin (*see pp. 44–7*). The story of Mackie's attempt to replicate Laphroaig is one of the most vainglorious stories in the history of Scotch – and this is a history not lacking in strange stories!

Ian Hunter set about selling Laphroaig as a single malt in the USA during the 1920s (even though such sales

51

LAPHROAIG'S PAGODAS
The pagoda roofs topping the malt kilns at Laphroaig were installed in the early 1920s, when Ian Hunter embarked on an ambitious expansion and remodelling of the site. Prior to this the distillery had a single kiln, topped with a cowl which turned with the wind, helping to draw the heat through the bed of green malt. Cowls like this are still used in oast houses today for drying hops.

were prohibited at the time) and while he was abroad the distillery was managed by his secretary, Bessie Williamson. When Hunter died in 1954, he bequeathed Laphroaig to her, along with the family's closely guarded 'distilling secrets'. These were considered so valuable that the company had tried to block publication of a memoir by a former cooper at the distillery – Mr James Whittaker – lest he divulge too much.

When Bessie took over, the distillery was in dire need of repair and in order to raise money she sold one-third of her shares to the Schenley Corporation of America. In 1967 she expanded the distillery to five stills, but though she was to remain its Managing Director until 1972, Schenley had acquired complete ownership by 1970. Laphroaig was to become an item on the balance sheet of several multinational corporations before becoming part of the Japanese distiller Suntory in 2014, where it is part of the Beam Suntory division.

DRYING THE MALT

Laphroaig is one of only nine distilleries with its own traditional floor maltings. Malting is the process which breaks down cell walls in the barleycorns by steeping them in water, with periodic air rests, then spreading them out on a concrete floor to germinate (this takes about a week, depending on the season). Once germinated, the malt – now called 'green malt' – is spread on the perforated metal floor of the kiln and dried; first by peat, then by hot air.

The malt-man operating the kiln that dries the green malt runs it as cool as possible. He is looking for smoke, not heat and will hose the peat fire with water if flames appear. At Laphroaig they burn peat for 15–16 hours, then switch to hot air from an oil-fired burner for a further 17–19 hours to complete the job.

53

Inverness

Tomatin

River Spey

Loch Ness

Dalwhinnie

Grampian Mountains

Blair Athol Edradour

Aberfeldy

River Tay

Dundee

Glenturret

Tullibardine

River Forth

Firth of Forth

Deanston

Stirling

Glengoyne

Edinburgh

Glasgow

River Clyde

CENTRAL HIGHLANDS

The landscape of the Central Highlands is intensely romantic; deep glens and shimmering lochs sit among magnificent mountains. The fertile alluvial glens carved by the River Tay and its tributaries, the Earn and the Tummel, attracted the attention of early farmer-distillers and later kindred spirits followed their example. Barley grows easily in the lush valleys and there is a rich supply of both water and peat. The region has never been officially sub-divided, but during the 19th century blenders began to refer to distinct whisky districts within the region, such as the 'malts of Perthshire'. The city of Perth emerged as the 'blending capital' of Scotland, with easy access to the Highlands for malt whisky fillings and the Lowlands for grain whisky and markets. Today, the Central Highlands stretches from Loch Lomond and the Trossachs in the south, across the Stirling plain to the Ochil Hills, taking in fertile Strathearn and mountainous Badenoch.

The malts from this area tend to be lighter-bodied and sweeter than other Highlanders and fragrant with blossom, fruit, honey and spice.

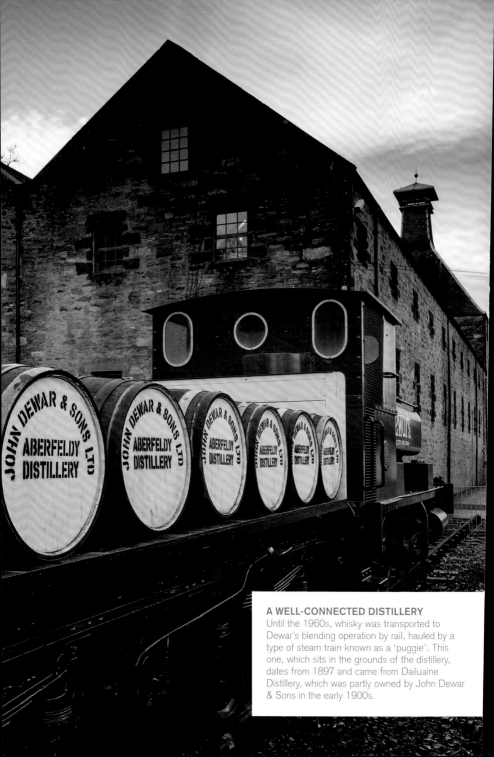

A WELL-CONNECTED DISTILLERY
Until the 1960s, whisky was transported to Dewar's blending operation by rail, hauled by a type of steam train known as a 'puggie'. This one, which sits in the grounds of the distillery, dates from 1897 and came from Dailuaine Distillery, which was partly owned by John Dewar & Sons in the early 1900s.

ABERFELDY

Honeycomb, melon, apples and pears

Aberfeldy PH15 2EB
www.dewars.com

Aberfeldy Distillery stands a quarter of a mile from the attractive village of Aberfeldy in the depths of Highland Perthshire. It owes its beginnings to the legendary John Dewar, who was born to a crofting family in 1806 and lured to the bright lights of Perth as a young man. He trained as a wine merchant, then went on to open his own wine and spirits business before focussing on blending and bottling whisky. By the time he died in 1880, John Dewar & Sons was ranked among the 'big three' blending houses.

The company was taken over by Dewar's sons, John Alexander and Tommy, who decided to build a distillery. The site chosen was only two miles from the croft in which their father had been born and the land had once been home to a brewery and a small distillery. They leased the site from the Marquess of Breadalbane, who retained the right to pan for gold in the Pitilie Burn, which was to supply the distillery with water.

The rags to riches story of John Dewar & Sons is probably the most colourful of any whisky company, largely owing to the remarkable talents of the 'Sons'. John Alexander (later Lord Forteviot) was responsible for the blending, while Tommy (who became Lord Dewar of Homestall) excelled at sales. Aged only 21, he travelled to London to tap contacts for business, but one had died and the other gone bankrupt, so he set about visiting pubs to ask for Dewar's by name. By 1892 he was thinking globally and embarked on a world tour to promote the whisky.

Alexander Cameron was the company's first Master Blender, and during the 1890s he conducted a number of experiments in mixing the malt and grain components of his blends separately, allowing them to 'marry' for several months before being blended together. The completed blend was then returned to casks for further marrying before bottling. This is time-consuming and therefore expensive, but the technique has been used by Dewar's blenders ever since, helping Dewar's White Label to become one of the world's bestselling whiskies. In 1998 John Dewar & Sons was bought by the Bacardi Corporation.

THE STILL HOUSE ▲
Aberfeldy's current still house was added in 1972–3 and in the process the two original stills were replaced with four precise copies. At the time, Aberfeldy and John Dewar's were owned by the Distillers Company Ltd and managed by its production division, Scottish Malt Distillers (SMD). The still-house design was known as the 'Waterloo Street' style, after the Glasgow address of SMD's engineering department. Its key feature is a glass exterior wall, with windows which could be opened, making for light and airy working conditions.

◄ A MODEL DISTILLERY
Aberfeldy was designed by Charles Cree Doig, the leading distillery architect of the late 19th century, when he was working at the height of his powers. He designed the distillery according to 'the most modern principles': – barley went in at one end, was converted into malt in the middle, then fermented and distilled and emerged as spirit. The Pitilie Burn, which supplies the distillery's process and cooling water, is shown in the foreground of the picture on this page.

THE VISITORS' CENTRE ▲

'Dewar's World of Whisky' visitor centre opened in 2000 and welcomes around 35,000 visitors a year. It has won many awards and makes excellent use of the outstanding Dewar archive to tell the story of the remarkable Dewar brothers and the global success of their blended Scotch whisky. The exit from the display is constructed from old barrel staves.

BLENDING AND BOTTLING ▶

Dewar's owes its success both to the quality of its malts and blends and to the marketing genius of Tommy Dewar. One of his many imaginative schemes was to place messages promising a 'Dewar's whisky reward' inside bottles, then throw them overboard while travelling by ship.

AN OLD-TIMER
Blair Athol is one of a handful of distilleries that were founded in the
18th century. The ivy-clad buildings that cluster around the courtyard
date back to the 1820s. Most of the distillery's output goes into
blended whisky, but a 12-year-old single malt, 'Flora and Fauna',
can be purchased at the visitor centre.

BLAIR ATHOL

Rich and malty, with nuts and dried fruits

Perth Road, Pitlochry, Perthshire PH16 5LY
www.discovering-distilleries.com

Blair Athol Distillery is a charming collection of grey stone buildings in the picturesque town of Pitlochry, Perthshire. Surrounded by mountains, the town sits at the foot of Ben Vrackie, the 'speckled mountain', whose slopes were at one time covered with white quartz. Springs on the mountain supply the distillery via the Allt Dour, 'the burn of the otter'.

There have been distillers in the area since at least the 17th century and it is said that 'the mellow barley bree from the cavern of Ben Vrackie warmed the hearts and strengthened the arms of the Highlanders' when they defeated a government army at the Battle of Killicrankie, 12 miles to the south, in 1689. Following the defeat of another Highland army at the Battle of Culloden in 1746, George Robertson of Fascally is said to have hidden from government soldiers in a large oak tree and was revived by the whisky made at Aldour Farm. This became licensed as Aldour Distillery in 1798, but following rebuilding and expansion in 1825, the name was changed to Blair Athol. The tree in which George Robertson took refuge still stands close to the distillery today.

The founders of the distillery were John Stewart and Robert Robertson; the latter is thought to have been a descendant of Robertson of Fascally. They were helped by their landlord, the Duke of Atholl, whose family home was Blair Castle, Blair Atholl (a village near the distillery with a slightly different spelling). The family still occupy the fortified house, the earliest parts of which date from the 12th century. In 1844 Queen Victoria granted the 6th Duke the unique privilege of having his own regiment, the Atholl Highlanders, which exists to this day.

By 1827 the distillery was controlled by Alexander Connacher, whom the novelist Sir Walter Scott described as 'one of the descendants of the chivalrous young Connacher, who was the early companion and admirer of Catherine Glover, the Fair Maid of Perth'. The distillery gained a great reputation, and as early as 1867, the legendary whisky blender Arthur Bell reported to a customer that the best whiskies he bought in were from 'Glenlivet, Pitlochry and Stirlingshire districts'. In years to come, the fortunes of the distillery would be inextricably linked to that of Arthur Bell & Sons.

61

In the early 1880s, Blair Athol was bought by Peter Mackenzie & Co, an Edinburgh blending house, who again expanded and modernized it. Mackenzie & Co was bought by Arthur Bell & Sons in 1933, giving them control of Blair Athol and Dufftown distilleries. With this acquisition Bell's moved from being a small local blender to being a medium-sized distiller with the potential to become a major player.

During the 1930's economic depression, Blair Athol was mothballed and it remained so until 1949 when Bell's refurbished and tastefully restored the old ivy-clad buildings as the brand home of Bell's Extra Special.

The company doubled capacity at Blair Athol to four stills, and by 1970,

Bell's was the bestselling Scotch in the UK. Around the same time, Bell's installed a visitor centre – Blair Athol had officially become the 'spiritual home of Bell's' and Pitlochry is very popular with tourists. The centre was substantially expanded in 1987 to include many new features, including a smuggler's still and now attracts around 35,000 visitors a year.

Between 1970 and 1980, Bell's sales in the UK increased from £20 million to £159 million. Such success attracted predators and in 1985 the company was subject to a hostile takeover by Guinness PLC. Two years later Guinness bought the Distillers Company Ltd (DCL), which later became part of Diageo, the owners of Blair Athol today.

BLAIR CASTLE
Blair Athol Distillery is around 7 miles north of Blair Atholl village, which is the site of Blair Castle, seat of the Dukes of Atholl. The castle also acts as headquarters for the world's most exclusive whisky club, The Keepers of the Quaich.

▲ THE STILL HOUSE

The distillery's spacious still house was reconstructed and expanded from two to four stills in 1949.They are onion-style stills that are run hot, with after-coolers, so as to achieve the heavy style of spirit that is desired.

RACKED WAREHOUSE ▶

Blair Athol is mainly matured in ex-bourbon refill hogsheads, but the robustness of the spirit makes it suitable for maturation in ex-sherry butts and these are used for the single malt bottlings released by its owner. The majority of the spirit is taken away to be matured in the Central Belt (between the Highlands and the Southern Uplands of Scotland), but some remains on site, in racked warehouses.

DALWHINNIE

Smooth, with heather honey

Dalwhinnie, Inverness-shire PH19 1AA
www.discovering-distilleries.com

Dalwhinnie is said to be 'the meeting place' of the drove roads coming out of Strathspey and those from the northwest Highlands. They combine here to head south to the great cattle markets at Crieff and Falkirk. The rough tracks used by the drovers were transformed into military roads in the 1730s by General George Wade, who held the auspicious title of 'Commander in Chief of His Majesty's forces, castles, forts and barracks in North Britain.'

Dalwhinnie has long been known as 'the highest distillery in Scotland,' though in reality Braeval now beats it by a couple of metres. It sits in a remote spot and was once notably described by a visitor as a 'desolate, wind-sliced, rain-lashed patch of Highland wilderness.' Despite this – or perhaps because of it – the whisky made here is named *spiorad sitheil*, 'the gentle (or peaceful) spirit' and the distillery's location is extremely romantic, surrounded as it is by high, heather-covered hills in an archetypically Highland setting.

The distillery was built by a small consortium of local men, who collectively called themselves the Strathspey Distillery Co Ltd and was designed by Charles Cree Doig, the famous distillery architect. It went into production in 1898, but closed almost immediately, owing to the general downturn in the industry. It was sold in 1905 to Cook & Bernheimer, the largest distillers in America at the time, becoming the first Scottish distillery to come under foreign ownership. They handed operations to their subsidiary company, James Munro & Sons Ltd, but in fact only owned the distillery for 14 years, before selling it to the well-known blenders Macdonald Greenlees. In 1926 it was acquired by the Distillers Company Ltd (DCL).

In 1986 the traditional worm tubs used to condense the spirit were replaced by modern shell-and-tube condensers – as happened with most distilleries in the post-war period – but this so changed the style of the spirit that the worms were reinstated in 1995. The high distillery is also used as a meteorological observation point and the manager treks across the lawn daily to check the Stevenson Screen (shown on the next page) – a screened wooden box that houses state-of-the-art weather instruments.

BRIDGE OVER THE RIVER TRUIM
General Wade directed the construction of 30 bridges in the Highlands and 240 miles of road in order to police the unruly Highlanders. On one of his bridges there is the charming epithet: 'If you had been here before I was made/You would lift up your hands and bless General Wade'! The fast-flowing River Truim, which runs through the village of Dalwhinnie, rises in the Drumochter Pass and flows into the Spey south of Newtonmore.

▲ SURROUNDED BY MOUNTAINS

Dalwhinnie lies 326 metres above sea level, in a glen surrounded by the Monadhliath Mountains, the Forest of Atholl, the Cairngorms and the Grampians. It is probably Scotland's coldest distillery, with an average annual temperature of only 60°C and has often found itself snowbound for several weeks during the winter.

CLIMATOLOGICAL STATION ▶

On account of its altitude and remote situation, Dalwhinnie Distillery has operated as a 'Climatological Station' since 1973. Every day, including Christmas and New Year, readings of temperature, wind strength, humidity, visibility, frost and hours of sunshine are recorded and sent to Edinburgh. This used to be the (unpaid!) job of the manager, but is now shared with other members of staff.

VAST STILLS
Dalwhinnie's two stills are unusually large: the wash-still is charged with 17,500 litres and the spirit still with 16,200 litres, providing plenty of contact between the alcohol vapour and the copper, making for a light spirit. This lightness is counterbalanced by the vapour being condensed in worm tubs, which deliver a full-bodied spirit.

AN INNOVATIVE MILL

Deanston was built as a cotton mill in 1785 by Richard Arkwright.
Known as the Adelphi Mill, it was driven by water drawn from the
River Teith, which powered four massive waterwheels. Today, the
distillery uses the same water source to drive hydroelectric turbines,
which provide all the distillery's electrical power and still manage to
pass on 75 per cent of the electricity they produce to the national grid.

DEANSTON

Malty, fruity and nutty

Doune FK16 6AG
www.deanstonmalt.com

Deanston was built in 1785 as a cotton mill by Richard Arkwright, who is often described as the 'Father of the Industrial Revolution' because he invented the modern factory system. His cotton mill combined power (in this case water power), machinery, semi-skilled labour and a novel material – cotton – to create mass-produced yarn. He also improved upon the Spinning Jenny to produce the Spinning Frame, which proved revolutionary in the development of British textiles.

Arkwright built the mill in the village of Doune, which is also home to a magnificent 14th-century castle that was built for Robert Stewart, Duke of Albany. The village is bounded to the south by the River Teith, which provided water-power for the mill. Arkwright's drive for improved efficiency led him to become the first person to use James Watt's steam engine to power textile equipment – he used the engine to pump water from the Teith to the millrace of the waterwheel. Given all this innovation, it is not surprising that the mill was described in the *First Statistical Account* (1782) as having 'the most perfect machinery in the kingdom'. The *Account* goes on

to explain why Arkwright built a mill in Scotland: 'The English had annoyed Sir Richard so much by invading his invention, he resolved to instruct young Scotsmen in the art, in preference to his own countrymen'. Under Arkwright's regime there were two 13-hour shifts per day, which overlapped. Bells rang at 5am and 5pm, and the gates were shut precisely at 6am and 6pm. Anyone who was late was not allowed to work that day and would be docked a day's pay.

The mill passed through several hands until it ceased production in 1965, when the fine stone buildings caught the eye of the Glasgow blenders Brodie Hepburn, owners of Tullibardine (at Blackford, not far away) and Macduff Distilleries. They formed a partnership with the owners of the mill to create a distillery at a time when the whisky trade was booming. Their first thought had been to use the echoing empty halls simply for maturing casks, but the availability of first-class process water from streams high in the Trossachs, combined with two working turbines (one dating from the 1920s) powered by water from the River Teith, caused them to change their minds and instead install a distillery.

FROM WEAVING SHED TO WAREHOUSE
Once used to house hundreds of rattling cotton Spinning Frames, operated by hundreds of poorly paid workers at the dawn of the Industrial Revolution, the vaulted rooms now hold hundreds of peacefully slumbering casks of malt whisky.

The conversion work, which involved removing four solid floors to create the still house, was completed in 10 months and production commenced in October 1969. The original plan was for Deanston to become the core malt in a blended Scotch named 'Old Bannockburn' but this never happened and in 1972 Brodie Hepburn sold to Invergordon Distillers.

The distillery was silent from 1982 to 1990, when it was sold to Burn Stewart Distillers for £2.1 million in cash and brought back into production. In 2012 it featured in Ken Loach's film *The Angels' Share*. The nearby Doune Castle (*opposite*) has also shown up in a movie, when it was used as Camelot, Castle Anthrax and Swamp Castle in *Monty Python and the Holy Grail* (1974).

▲ THE MASH TUN

Deanston has several traditional features, including the cast-iron rake-and-plough mash tun; eight Corton steel washbacks; and brass chokers round the necks of its two boil-ball-style stills. Here mash-man Andy Scott is 'mashing in' (mixing the barley grist with hot water as it enters the mash tun).

▲ THE RIVER TEITH AND DOUNE CASTLE

'Dean' and 'Doune' both derive from 'dun', meaning 'a hill fort'. Doune Castle, just up river from Deanston Distillery, is one of the largest and best-preserved examples of medieval military-domestic architecture in Scotland. In the late 1500s it was the seat of James Stewart, 'The Bonnie Earl of Moray', who was famously murdered by a rival, the Earl of Huntly, in 1592. According to Sir Walter Scott, Huntly slashed Moray across the face and Moray's dying words were 'Ye hae spilt a better face than yer ain' ('You have spoiled a better face than your own').

EDRADOUR

Robust, floral and fruity

Pitlochry, Perthshire PH16 5JP
www.edradour.com

For decades, Edradour was the smallest distillery in Scotland and although it can no longer claim this distinction, it remains one of the neatest, most compact and most traditional. It is not surprising that such an attractive place is among the most visited distilleries in Scotland, attracting around 60,000 people each year.

Edradour is a classic example – perhaps *the* classic example – of the size and style of the 'farm' distilleries that were found all over Scotland until the whisky boom of the 1890s, when larger units were required to meet demand. The distillery was built in 1837 by a group of seven farmers on a strip of land beside the Edradour Burn, which they had leased from the Duke of Atholl. One of the group was Duncan Forbes, who had established a tiny distillery in 1825, possibly on the same site.

Descendants of the founding farmers owned the distillery until 1933, when they were forced to sell because of dramatically falling cask sales. The new owner was William Whitely & Co and the price was £1,050, including two cottages. Whitely was a tough Yorkshireman who had started work as a sales representative for a wine and spirits company, but was dismissed for 'going beyond his remit.' In 1914 he had bought the Leith wine and spirits merchant, J G Turney & Son, selling mainly to export markets. Turney's was a key customer of Edradour and used the whisky in its House of Lords and King's Ransom blends – the latter was introduced in 1928 and was allegedly shipped round the world before being offered for sale. On account of this it was reputedly the most expensive Scotch of its day.

In 1920, Prohibition arrived in America, which was Turney's leading market, but William Whitely was unperturbed. He appointed gangster Frank Costello as his 'US Sales Consultant' on an annual salary of £3,300. Costello was a leading mafioso (he was the model for Mario Puzo's *The Godfather*) and a major bootlegger; he controlled numerous speakeasies and clubs in New York City. Costello may also have been responsible for naming Whitely 'the Dean of Distilling.' In 1937, Costello's sidekick – Irving Haim – bought J J Dailey & Sons, the holding company for William Whitely & Co, using funds provided by a mafioso group that included Costello. This made him owner of the distillery. As far as the whisky was concerned, Haim left

THE MALTINGS
The former malt barn has been converted into an attractive visitor centre; the kiln, with its pagoda roof, is still intact but not used.

things as they were (except for installing electricity in 1948), as did his successor, Campbell Distillers, who acquired Edradour in 1986. The single malt was first bottled by its new owners in 1990.

In 2002 Edradour was bought by Andrew Symington, owner of the well-known independent bottler Signatory Vintage Scotch Whisky. He has made many improvements to the site, including building a bottling hall (2007) and a large new warehouse (2010) incorporating 'Caledonia Hall', a function suite. However, he has not changed Edradour's ancient stills (the wash still dates from 1881) or worm tubs and the distillery has the only remaining Morton Refrigerator.

OLD FARM BUILDINGS

The distillery is in the hamlet of Balnauld, sitting above the town of Pitlochry. It uses water that stems from Moulin Moor, which is rich in peat and granite. The old lime-washed and red-painted farm buildings that make up the distillery are home to the smallest stills permissible under Customs and Excise regulations.

THE LOST DISTILLERY OF BALLECHIN

Between 1810 and 1927 there was a distillery near Edradour called Ballechin. Today Andrew Symington uses this name for a peaty expression of Edradour, casks of which are racked in the warehouse.

A WASH CALLED 'JOE'

Wash, the sweet liquid produced when the worts are fermented, is like a strong ale (around 8% vol) and it is known by distillery workers as 'Joe'. In days gone by it was not uncommon to 'sample' the Joe, but those daring folks had to be careful, because it is a rapidly acting diuretic.

GLENGOYNE

Malty, fruity, nutty

Dumgoyne, Glasgow G63 9LB
www.glengoyne.com

Glengoyne Distillery straddles the Highland Line: its distillery sits in the Highland region, while its warehouses lie across the road in the Lowlands. Until the 1970s the malt was classified as a Lowland whisky, although light, but today the style of the make is definitely Highland, as is the surrounding landscape. The 'Highland Line' was introduced in 1784 and it was really a notional frontier for excise tax purposes, allowing different duties and other provisos on either side of the Line. Broadly speaking, the Line ran diagonally across Scotland from Dumbarton on the River Clyde to Aberdeen on the east coast.

Glengoyne Distillery was founded in 1833 by the local landowner and was originally named Burnfoot of Dumgoyne. When the lease was taken up by the Lang Brothers in 1876, they changed the name to Glen Guin and this was its name when Alfred Barnard 'inspected' (to use his own term) the place around 1885. He noted the following: 'the distillery is situated at the foot of Dumgoyne and just below a romantic waterfall 50 feet in height, which supplies all the water used in the works... The annual output is 45,000 gallons of pure alcohol.' Barnard also observes that 'the spirits are distilled three times', as was the practice in many Lowland distilleries, although this one had only two stills.

In 1861, Alexander and Gavin Lang began trading as whisky blenders from the Argyll Free Church in Oswald Street, Glasgow, which they later took over and turned into a bonded warehouse. They initially used the church basement, giving rise to the saying: 'The spirits below were the spirits of wine and the spirits above were the spirits divine.' Their successors continued to own the company and distillery until 1965, when they sold both to Robertson & Baxter, whisky brokers in Glasgow and sister company to Highland Distilleries (now both part of the Edrington Group). As part of a rationalization programme in 2003 focussing on 'core brands', Edrington sold Lang Bros and Glengoyne Distillery to Ian Macleod & Company, an independent company that owns Tamdhu, Isle of Skye and Smokehead Scotch whiskies, among others. The new owners have greatly increased the range and availability.

THE BLAIRGAR BURN

When the distillery was founded by the local
landowner, Edmondstone of Duntreath, it was named
'Burnfoot of Dumgoyne' on account of its location – it
sits in a narrow glen at the foot of the Blairgar Burn,
which tumbles down from the Campsie Fells behind.
The glen is Glen Guin, 'the Glen of the Wild Geese'
and this was the distillery's name from 1876 to 1905.

VENTILATING PAGODA

Glengoyne Distillery is a cluster of
picturesque white buildings, its maltings
topped by a pagoda-shaped ventilator
designed by arhictect Charles Cree Doig.
Long since surpassed by a modern ventilation
system, the pagoda was a groundbreaking
piece of design in the late 1800s, which
allowed smoke to escape while protecting
the drying malt below from rain and snow.

A LIGHTER SPIRIT

In 1966–7, Glengoyne was reconstructed and a third spirit still installed. This arrangement means that the low wines from the wash-still are split between two spirit stills, which run very slowly, making for a light style of spirit.

A HIGHLAND DISTILLERY
Standing on the edge of a wooded glen
among rolling Perthshire hills, Glenturret's
location is quintessentially Highland.

GLENTURRET

Nutty and malty, with fruits and a hint of smoke

The Hosh, Crieff PH7 4HA
www.theglenturret.com

Glenturret Distillery is situated on the west bank of the River Turret, in a wooded glen known as 'The Hosh' near Crieff, Perthshire. The distillery claims to be the oldest in Scotland, based on the fact that there was a farm distillery in The Hosh in the 1770s. However, private distilling was perfectly legal prior to 1781, providing the spirits were not offered for sale and many early licensed distilleries were founded on sites previously owned by smugglers, so other distilleries may dispute this claim.

The first license to distil in The Hosh was granted to one John Drummond. He continued until he ran out of money in 1842; his successor also went bust in 1874, as did the next tenant (who immediately changed the name from 'Hosh' to the more attractive 'Glenturret') in 1903. Glenturret was then taken over by a company that went into liquidation just 26 years later.

Enter James Fairlie, who bought the site in 1957, reinstated the equipment (often acquiring second-hand plant) and integrated new buildings with the old. His intention was to 'preserve the craft traditions of malt distilling and develop their appreciation', to which

end he opened Glenturret to the public. This was almost unheard of at the time: during the 1960s Glenfiddich was the only distillery that offered visitor facilities.

James Fairlie sold the distillery to the French distiller Rémy Cointreau in 1981 and they expanded the visitor facilities. In 1990 Highland Distillers, owners of the Famous Grouse brand since 1970, bought Glenturret Distillery and so the two names were joined for the first time. The Famous Grouse blend is made up of whisky from Glenrothes (*see pp. 204–7*), Macallan (*see pp. 212–15*) and Highland Park (*see pp. 234–7*), along with around 65 per cent grain whisky. It was created in 1897 by Matthew Gloag, owner of a modest grocery, wine and spirits store in Perth, who was selling around 40,000 cases of Famous Grouse per year when the brand was bought by Highland.

In 1998, Highland itself was bought by The 1887 Company Ltd, a partnership made up of the Edrington Group and William Grant & Sons. The new owners spent £2.2 million creating a visitor centre named 'The Famous Grouse Experience', which today welcomes around 100,000 people a year.

▲ **FAMOUS MOUSER**

Many distilleries have cats, because
traditionally they all had malt barns that were
alive with rats and mice. The most famous cat
of all is Towser, who looked after Glenturret
between 1963 and 1987 and slaughtered
28,899 mice, a fact reported in *The Guinness
Book of Records*.

▲ **THE FAMOUS GROUSE**

Grouse has been the bestselling blended
Scotch whisky in Scotland since 1983.
The famous whisky blend was first created
in 1897 by Matthew Gloag & Son, but
is now celebrated by the brand's current
owners, Edrington, in The Famous Grouse
Experience, winner of 2015's Whisky Visitor
Attraction of the Year (*Whisky* magazine).

ANCIENT METHODS
Glenturret retains a number of antique features, by design, but none more so than the mash tun, which is hand-stirred with a paddle. This is a uniquely surviving method from the deep past. The draff (husks and spent grains left after the mashing process has been completed) is also shovelled out by hand.

TRADITIONAL TOOLS
Wash-stills are fitted with 'sight glasses', so the operator can see how far up the neck of the still the liquid rises when it boils, then lower the heat to prevent it coming over into the condenser. In the days before heat-resistant glass was invented, the liquid level was measured by banging a wooden ball against the still neck and gauging the level by the sound it made.

TOMATIN

Sweet, with apples and nuts

Inverness IV13 7YT
www.tomatin.com

Tomatin Distillery stands at over 305 metres above sea level in rolling moorland, on the edge of the Monadhliath Mountains, 18 miles south of Inverness. The name is taken from the small village that grew up around the distillery and is thought to derive from the Gaelic term *tom-aiteann*, 'hillock of juniper'. Juniper was much prized by illicit distillers, because it gives off no smoke while burning, so it suited their secretive activity.

Whisky has been made on this site for a very long time, both in the 'Old Laird's House' that stands near the current distillery buildings (*see overleaf*) and in small, illicit stills around the district. These were able to take advantage of the area's remoteness and of its excellent water, which flows over quartz and granite, through peat and heather, and finally reaches the Allt na-Frith (the 'free burn'), a tributary of the River Findhorn.

The current distillery was built in 1897 by a group of local businessmen trading as the Tomatin Spey District Distillery Company Ltd, at the height of the late Victorian whisky boom. Like so many others, it faced severe difficulties when that boom turned to bust around 1900. The company went into liquidation in 1905 and the distillery closed, but only for four years, until it was revived by the New Tomatin Distillers Company Ltd.

An additional pair of stills joined the original ones in 1956; two more in 1958, four in 1961, one in 1963 and a further 12 in 1974, when a dark-grains plant was also built to process the residues (spent grains and pot ale) into cattle food.

At 23 stills – 12 wash- and 11 spirit – Tomatin was then the largest distillery in Scotland, but it only operated to its full capacity of 13.5 million litres of pure alcohol for a few years. Production was cut dramatically during the 1980s and Tomatin Distillers went into liquidation in 1986. The distillery was sold to the Japanese companies Takara Shuzo and Okura, who were both long-standing customers. They jointly formed Tomatin Distillery Company Ltd. This was the first time Japanese companies had entered the Scotch whisky industry. In 1997–8, 11 stills were removed and the dark-grains plant was closed. Around 2000, Okura's share in the distillery was acquired by the Marubeni Corporation, one of Japan's leading integrated trading companies and the consortium was joined by the 300-year-old Kokubu & Company Ltd.

▲ **THE OLD LAIRD'S HOUSE**
Tomatin Distillery was situated on a drove road and it is said that thirsty drovers filled their flasks with whisky from a private still in the 'Old Laird's House' (which still stands close to the distillery) as early as the 15th century.

◄ **A LARGE, EFFICIENT DISTILLERY**
The spacious interior of Tomatin Distillery once housed 23 stills and during the mid-1970s had the largest capacity of any malt distillery in Scotland. At the time it was redesigned to be highly efficient and this attitude prevails today – in 2013 the distillery fitted a biomass steam boiler, reducing carbon emissions by 80 per cent.

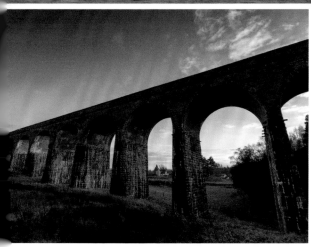

▲ HAUNTED BY HOBGOBLINS

Tomatin's utilitarian appearance is in marked contrast to the surrounding country, which is wild, remote and periodically haunted by the *Cu Bochan*, 'the hobgoblin dog'. Some years ago it was reported that a distillery worker was 'relentlessly pursued' by a fearful black beast, 'steam spiralling from flared nostrils and teeth bared'.

▲ TOMATIN VIADUCT

The main line connecting Inverness and the Highlands to the south runs over an elegant viaduct close to the distillery. It was built by the Highland Railway Company, which itself was formed by merger with, among others, the Great North of Scotland Railway (known locally as 'a really terrible company with a very grand name'!).

TULLIBARDINE

Sweet, fruity and malty

Stirling Street, Auchterarder, Perthshire PH4 1QG
www.tullibardine.com

The village of Blackford, where stands Tullibardine Distillery, has long been famous for its water. The early habitation here grew up around a ford across the Allan Water, where, so tradition has it, the 'Fair Queen Helen', wife of a 12th-century Norwegian king, was drowned while attempting to cross during a spate. She was buried nearby at Deaf Knowe; a stone marks the spot and the river's name may derive from hers – 'Allan' from 'Helen'. The event also gave the village its name, 'Black Ford'.

The site is also famous for brewers and distillers – the first public brewery in Scotland was established here. Known as Sharp's Brewery, it supplied ale to King James IV in 1488, when he was returning to Stirling after his coronation at Scone, near Perth. For this reason, every bottle of Tullibardine bears a crown and the date 1488. The water used for the local beer came from a spring in the Ochil Hills; today, this water is bottled under the Highland Spring brand and used as process water for the Tullibardine Distillery, which collects it from the nearby Danny Burn.

Tullibardine Distillery was built on the site of Sharp's Brewery and takes its name from nearby Tullibardine Moor, now famous for the championship golf courses attached to Gleneagles Hotel. This was once owned by the powerful Murray family, whose seat, Tullibardine Castle, has long ceased to exist. However, the chapel they built in 1424 is today considered to be one of the most complete medieval churches in Scotland.

The site of the old Sharp's Brewery was bought in 1947 by William Delmé-Evans, a Welsh land surveyor with an interest in brewing and distilling. He designed the distillery while recovering from tuberculosis contracted during World War II and then managed the distillery after it opened in 1949. It was the first new distillery to be built since 1900 and Delmé-Evans was a pioneer of distillery efficiency; his production facilities were well ahead of the times in terms of energy efficiency and conservation. After selling Tullibardine to the Glasgow blenders Brodie Hepburn in 1953 due to continuing health problems, he would go on to design Jura (*see pp. 238–41*), Macduff and Glenallachie distilleries.

In 1971 Tullibardine was bought by Invergordon Distillers, which was itself acquired by Whyte & Mackay

A NEW DESIGN
Tullibardine was designed and built in the 1940s by William Delmé-Evans, who played an important part in the modernization of the Scotch whisky industry.

in 1993. The distillery was then mothballed for ten years before being sold to a consortium of whisky men who resumed production. They raised the money to do this by acquiring ground adjacent to the distillery for development into an upmarket retail park, then selling it to a leading property developer. Having got Tullibardine up and running again, the consortium then sold it to the family-owned French wine and spirits company Maison Michel Picard, owner of Chassagne-Montrachet (among others) in Burgundy. The new owners introduced 20- and 25-year-old bottlings and simplified the malts to three core finishes.

◀ A COMPACT DISTILLERY

Tullibardine is very compact, all stages of
production taking place in close proximity
to each other. It has nine stainless steel
washbacks (foreground), a stainless steel full-
Lauter mash tun (mid-ground) and two spirit
stills (background).

▲ BY ROYAL APPROVAL

It is said that King James IV stopped at
the Blackford brewery to buy ale after his
coronation. A wrought-iron gate in one of the
warehouses records the year as 1488. James
IV was Scotland's greatest Renaissance
prince, a patron of the arts, fascinated by
medicine and science (including distilling)
and founder of the first faculty of medicine in
Britain, within the University of Aberdeen.

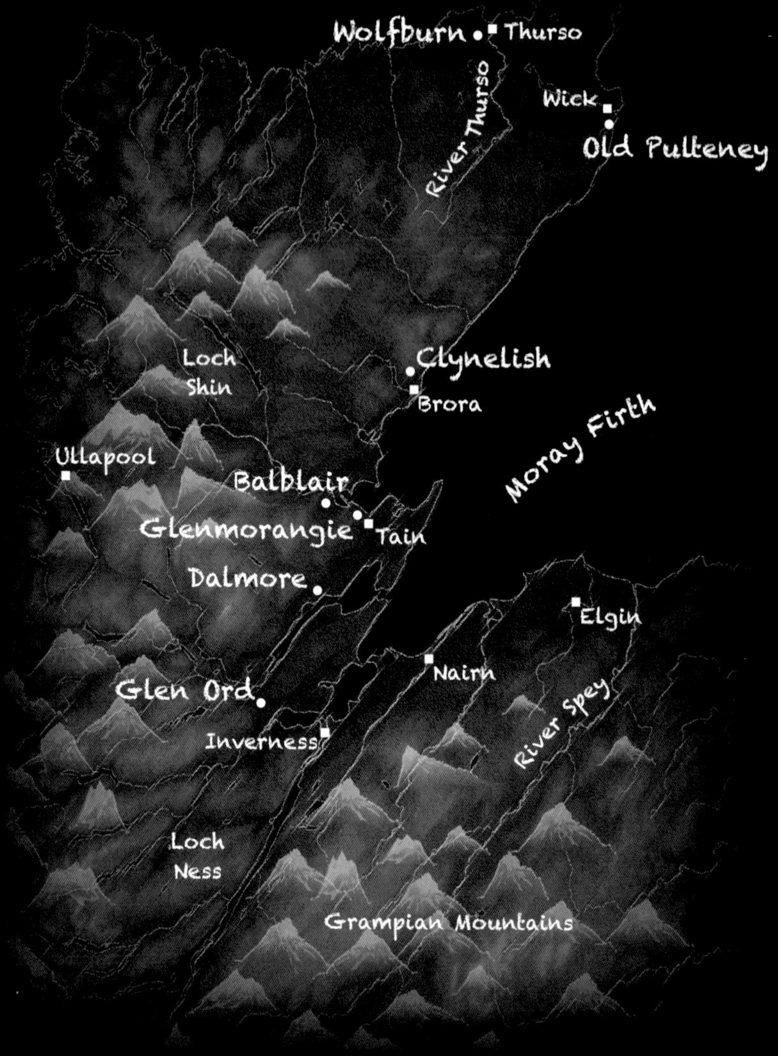

Wolfburn ● ■ Thurso

River Thurso

Wick ■

Old Pulteney

Loch
Shin

Clynelish
●
■ Brora

Ullapool ■

Balblair
●

Glenmorangie ■ Tain
●

Moray Firth

Dalmore ●

Elgin ■

Nairn ■

River Spey

Glen Ord ●

Inverness ■

Loch
Ness

Grampian Mountains

whisky, giving it a noticeable saltiness. In general these whiskies are complex, medium-bodied and sometimes spicy and lightly smoky.

THE FAR NORTH RAILWAY LINE

Like very many other distilleries, the 'new' Balblair was relocated to take advantage of the railway line which had recently been constructed between Inverness and Thurso, off which a siding was built to handle incoming coal and barley and outgoing casks of whisky.

BALBLAIR

Grapes, honeycomb and a trace of smoke

Edderton, Tain, Ross-Shire IV19 1LB
www.balblair.com

The first licensed distillery at Balblair can make a good claim to be one of the earliest in the Highlands. Official records say it was founded around 1790 by one John Ross, but it may be considerably earlier: beer was being brewed on the site in 1749. Alfred Barnard, the indefatigable distillery-bagger, wrote in 1887: 'In former days the whole neighbourhood abounded in illicit smuggling bothies and was the scene of many a struggle between the revenue officers and the smugglers.'

The distillery's location, in rolling farmland backed by heather-covered hills above the Dornoch Firth, is very attractive. The district is called Edderton; it is known as 'the parish of peats' and it is reputed to have the purest air in Scotland. In his monumental *Scotch Whisky Industry Record* (1987) Charles Craig described Balblair as 'one of the most attractive small distilleries still standing' and the description still holds good today.

Ross's descendant Andrew Ross had moved the distillery to its present location, half a mile to the north, around 1872, in order to take advantage of the recently constructed railway line. He expanded it in 1894 before deciding to move to Pollo Distillery near Tain just two years later.

The tenancy of Balblair was taken over by Alexander Cowan, but he went bankrupt in 1910 and the distillery was closed until 1947 when it was bought by a solicitor from Banff, Robert Cumming. Known to many people simply as 'Bertie', Cumming also acquired Old Pulteney Distillery at Wick. He expanded the Balblair site, then sold Balblair and Pulteney to the Canadian distiller, Hiram Walker. In 1988, Hiram Walker joined Allied Distillers, who sold Balblair to its current owners, Inver House Distillers Ltd, in 1996.

The malt whisky was not bottled by the distillery owners until 2000, when Inver House began to release limited amounts in a series named 'Elements' (a reference to the purity of the air). Since 2007, the single malt has been bottled in limited edition 'vintages' from selected casks, labelled by year not by age, but with a 'rolling core' of three vintages – at around 30, 20 and 10 years old – together with occasional single cask bottlings.

CLYNELISH

Candlewax, heather pollen and scented smokes

Clynelish Road, Brora, Highlands and Islands KW9 6LR
www.discovering-distilleries.com

In 1896, *Harpers Wine and Spirit Gazette* reported: 'The make [from Clynelish] has always obtained the highest price of any single Scotch whisky. It is sent out, duty paid, to private customers all over the kingdom; and it also commands a very valuable export trade: the demand for it in that way is so great that the proprietors... have for many years been obliged to refuse trade orders.' The skilled distillers at Clynelish were producing single malt only, turning down orders from blending houses.

I know of no other Scotch malt whisky where this was the case: at the time, the vast majority of distillers sent their entire annual output for blending. The excellence of the make from Clynelish Distillery was confirmed by the great wine connoisseur Professor George Saintsbury in his *Notes to a Cellar Book* (1921) where he lists it among only five malts for special praise.

The distillery, which stands on the edge of the pretty seaport of Brora in the far northeast of Scotland, was founded in 1819 by the local laird, the Marquess of Stafford (later 1st Duke of Sutherland) as part of his plan to 'improve' his wife's vast northern estates. This plan also required the clearing of some 15,000 tenants from the land to make way for sheep, which became known as the infamous 'Sutherland Clearances.' Some of those 'cleared' were moved to coastal townships like Brora and encouraged to take up fishing – or, in this case, to become distillers.

It was generally hoped that the establishment of a legal distillery would put an end to the widespread smuggling in the district – a practice which had, in the words of James Loch, the estate's infamous Lands Commissioner, nursed the people 'in every species of deceit, vice, idleness and dissipation.' The original distillery owners still have a presence at Clynelish: a stone bearing the coats of arms of the Marquess of Stafford and the Countess of Sutherland, dated 1820, has been preserved in the gable end of the old still house.

BRORA AND CLYNELISH

The original Clynelish distillery, now closed, stands close to the current distillery, built in 1967–8 in the 'Waterloo Street' style applied by Scottish Malt Distillers to a dozen of their distilleries during the '60s and '70s. Most of the distillery buildings date from the 1890s and its warehouses are still used to mature spirit from the new distillery.

The distillery passed through the hands of several licensees and then in 1896, Clynelish was bought by the partnership of Ainslie & Co, blenders in Glasgow and John Risk, previously at Bankier Distillery. They rebuilt it and in 1925 it was bought by the Distillers Company Ltd (now Diageo) and licensed to John Walker & Sons. The distillery was mothballed from 1931 to 1939 and renamed 'Brora' in 1969, after the company's production division, Scottish Malt Distillers, built a new distillery adjacent to the old one and named this 'Clynelish' too. Brora was closed and dismantled in 1983, though the elegant old buildings remain and the warehouses are still used by Clynelish Distillery.

Between 1972 and 1974, Brora/Clynelish was making heavily peated spirit for blending purposes, to replace the make from Caol Ila Distillery on Islay, which was being rebuilt. A limited edition of the 1972 Brora was released by Diageo in 2014, priced at £7,000 – their most expensive single malt whisky to date. I can vouch for its excellence!

RIVERS OF GOLD ▼
The Brora is one of the top salmon rivers in Scotland and one of the few which has consistently increased catches over the years, thanks to excellent management. Clynelish draws its process water from the Clynemilton Burn. Both the burn and the Brora are famously rich in particles of gold and are popular with amateur gold panners.

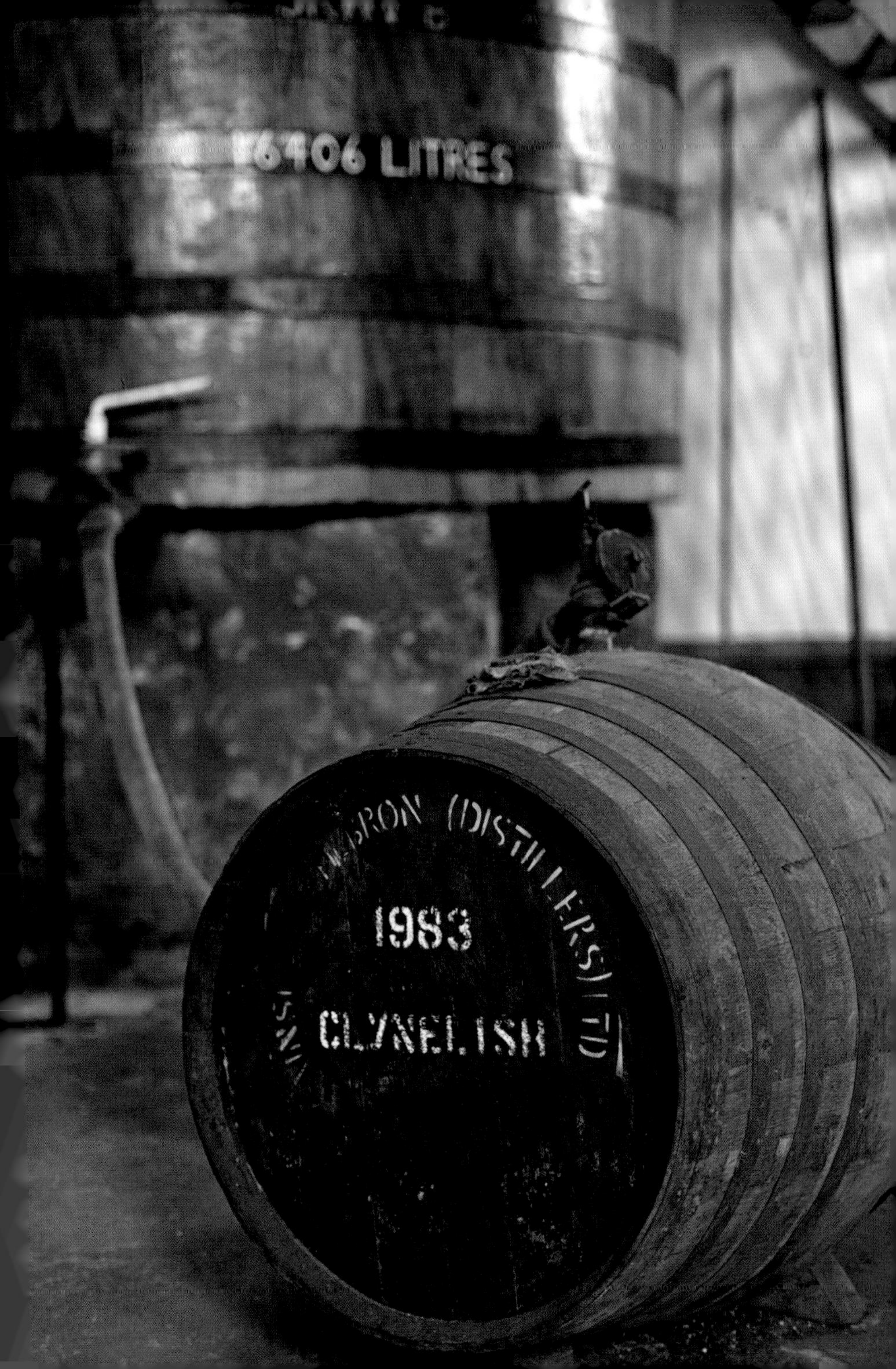
6406 LITRES
1983
CLYNELISH

DALMORE

Rich, with malt, fruitcake and orange peel

Alness, Highlands and Islands IV17 OUT
www.thedalmore.com

Dalmore Distillery, at Alness, overlooking the Cromarty Firth, was established in 1839 by Alexander Matheson, a partner in Jardine Matheson & Co, which became the largest foreign trading company in the Far East by the end of the 19th century. The firm had been founded seven years earlier by Alexander's uncle, James Matheson and William Jardine, both graduates of Edinburgh University. Their early fortunes were made in the opium trade with China and during the 1830s the partners diversified into tea, spices, sugar, cotton and silk: by 1841 the firm owned 19 fast intercontinental clipper ships, as well as hundreds of smaller vessels for inshore trade.

In 1845 Alexander Matheson bought Ardross Estate, which included Dalmore, from the Duke of Sutherland and appointed William Mackenzie as his factor (manager). In 1867, William's son Andrew (aged 24) and his younger brother Charles were granted the lease of the distillery. They and their descendants would manage Dalmore (and, after 1891, own it) for almost 100 years.

In 1960, the Mackenzies amalgamated with the famous Glasgow blenders, Whyte & Mackay, who have perpetuated the Mackenzie connection,

not only by including the family's crest on all their bottles, but by releasing bottlings such as The Dalmore King Alexander III, commemorating the origin of the crest.

Dalmore claims to have the oldest stills in the Highlands: part of one of them dates from 1874. The unusual combination of flat-topped wash-stills and four spirit stills (*see opposite page, below*) is augmented by size difference: one of the spirit stills is twice as large as the other three, producing a lighter, more citric and spicy spirit, while the other three produce a heavier style. This balance of light and heavy spirits gives Dalmore malt whisky its unique character.

During the 1990s and 2000s, two further malts – Dalmore Mackenzie 1992 and Dalmore Castle Leod – were released to raise money for the Mackenzie clan. The latter malt takes its name from Castle Leod in Strathpeffer, which is the home of the Earl of Cromartie, High Chief of Clan Mackenzie and reputed to be the oldest intact castle in Britain. In 2010, Dalmore Trinitas 64-year-old was the first malt whisky to sell for £100,000; only three bottles were filled, hence the name.

A PLEASING PROSPECT
The distillery has a fine position overlooking the northern shores of the Cromarty Firth. Its appearance has been compared with that of an old-fashioned country railway station and its offices are partly panelled with carved oak from a nearby shooting lodge.

◄ STILLS WITH A DIFFERENCE
The distilling regime is unique: the four wash-stills (*to the rear*) have flat tops, rather than swan necks, which makes for a more robust spirit, because the alcohol vapour has less contact with copper, while the four spirit stills have unusual water jackets around their necks. These were first fitted in 1839, to ensure that the copper is continually cooled, increasing reflux.

MORANGIE FARM

In 1843 a brewery on Morangie Farm was converted into a small distillery by William Matheson, but even as it grew in size the farm continued, distilling being considered an essential extension of the farming year during the winter months, providing fodder for livestock from the spent grains and residues.

GLENMORANGIE

Light, floral and citric

Tain, Ross-Shire, IV19 1PZ
www.glenmorangie.com

For many years Glenmorangie has been the bestselling malt whisky in Scotland, so it is perhaps surprising that until the late 1970s the vast majority of the make went for blending. It was only in 1979 that the company began to promote it as a single.

The distillery stands on the southern shore of the Dornoch Firth, near the Royal Burgh of Tain in Ross-shire. Tain is Scotland's oldest royal burgh, with a bishopric dating from the 9th century. The distillery was created in 1843 by William Matheson, part-owner of Balblair Distillery (*see pp. 94–5*)and a relation of Alexander Matheson, who founded Dalmore Distillery (*see pp. 100–1*).

Matheson built the distillery on the site of a brewery which had been operating since 1738. Within six years of opening, production had reached 90,000 litres of pure alcohol, which was a sizeable amount for the time; the distillery made good use of the barley grown locally on the fertile lands of Easter Ross. When whisky historian Alfred Barnard visited the site in around 1886, it was due to be rebuilt and he described the old distillery as 'certainly the most ancient and most primitive we have seen and now almost in ruins.'

William Matheson completed the rebuilding a year after Barnard's visit and in 1918 the distillery was bought by the partnership of Leith blending firm Macdonald & Muir and whisky brokers Durham & Company. By the late 1930s, whole ownership lay with Macdonald & Muir and remained so until 1996, when the company became a public company under the name of Glenmorangie. At this point the Macdonald family retired from the industry and sold their shares to Moët Hennessy.

The Glenmorangie Company has a long tradition of exploring wood influences. A former managing director, Neil McKerrow, commissioned pioneering research into the subject in 1986–7, when he began experimenting with 'wood finishing.' This was essentially the re-racking of whisky into ex-wine barrels for the final years of its maturation. The first expression to apply the technique was the 1963 Vintage, which was released in 1987, having been finished for 18 months in ex-oloroso butts. It was the first malt to use the term 'finishing' on the back label.

Although the *Inverness Advertiser* reported that casks of Glenmorangie were being sent to the Vatican, Italy and to San Francisco, USA in 1880, it was

THE STILL HOUSE

At 5.14 metres, the stills at Glenmorangie are the tallest in the industry and produce a light style of spirit. The earliest stills in this style were probably installed during the rebuilding of the distillery in 1887 and were said to have come from a gin distillery. The whisky's success since 1979 has led to steady expansion of capacity: from 2 to 4 stills in 1979, doubling to 8 stills in 1990 and increasing to 12 stills in 2008.

only in the late 1970s that Macdonald & Muir began to promote it as a single malt. In 1980 the number of stills was doubled to four and in 1981 a highly successful and creative print advertising campaign was launched, emphasizing the high craft that went into making the malt and humanizing it. Each advertisement featured woodcuts of the men themselves, from the distillery manager to the tractor driver, under the overall heading 'Crafted by the Sixteen Men of Tain'. Although Glenmorangie now employs nearly 400 people, the distillery workforce is still, they say, those 16 men.

THE SPIRIT SAFES
Glenmorangie's still house is reminiscent of a cathedral, with tall columns rising to right and left, creating a nave, at the end of which, in place of the altar, are the 12 brass spirit safes which allow the operator to direct the flow of spirit.

GLENMORANGIE FROM THE DORNOCH FIRTH
Described as 'one of the least well-known beauty spots in Scotland', the Dornoch Firth is a Special Protection Area (SPA), with a large number of resident waders and shore birds (including ospreys) and many winter visitors (including bar-tailed godwits, teal, wigeon and curlews by the hundred).

THE CADBOLL STONE

Not far from the distillery stands Glenmorangie House (formerly Cadboll House)
in its walled garden, beyond which is the pebble beach of the Tarbat Peninsula,
where stood the Hilton of Cadboll Stone, one of the most magnificently decorated
Pictish monuments. The original is now in the National Museum of Scotland, but it
has been replaced on site by a replica stone.

Carved around 800 CE, the landward side depicts a hunting scene surrounded by
an extremely intricate zoomorphic border, with further Pictish symbolism above and
below. The lower panel of complex, intertwined spirals, like a display of Catherine
wheels, has been adopted by Glenmorangie in their packaging.

THE FIONNAIDH BURN
Fionnaidh means 'white' and the White Burn that supplies Glen Ord Distillery with its process water is formed from the two 'waters of heaven and earth', providing a mix of spring and rain water.

GLEN ORD

Waxy, with dried orange peel, almonds and nougat

Old Road, Muir of Ord, Ross-shire IV6 7UJ
www.discovering-distilleries.com

Glen Ord is a classic example of the 'Highland' style and over the years has been released under a variety of brand names, including Glenordie, Ord, Ordie, Glen Oran and Muir of Ord. Since 2006 it has been enjoying considerable success in Asia as The Singleton of Glen Ord.

By 2013 it was numbered among the top 10 bestselling single malts worldwide, but this still accounts for less than 15 per cent of the distillery's output. During 2013–14 capacity was doubled (to 10 million litres per year), with six new stills, ten new washbacks and a new mash tun, all located in the former maltings.

Like so many others, the distillery on the edge of Muir of Ord occupies a site that was formerly very popular with smugglers. There were said to be more than 40 illicit stills in the district – though some sources claim only 10 – and the visitor centre has several of these old-timers on display, often dredged from lochs nearby. The two mountain lochs that supply the process water for Glen Ord are referred to locally as 'the waters of heaven and earth', because one is fed by rainwater, the other by springs. Their names in Gaelic are *Loch Nan Eun* ('The Loch of the Birds') and *Loch Nam Bonnach* ('The Loch of the Peats').

The distillery was founded in 1838 by Thomas Mackenzie, the local laird. The widow of the first licensee, Alexander McLennan, married another Mackenzie – a banker named Alexander – who built a new still house in 1878. Unfortunately it burned down the same year and he had to start again (Glen Ord was lit by paraffin lamps until 1949). In 1896 the distillery was sold to James Watson & Co, very well-known blenders in Dundee, who owned an additional three Highland distilleries. Watson's was acquired by John Dewar & Sons in 1923 and when they joined DCL in 1925, ownership passed to the larger company – and thus to Diageo, its successor.

▲ THE OLD MALTINGS

Ord Distillery used to operate its own floor maltings and dry green malt in its own pagoda-topped kilns. In 1968 a large new mechanical maltings was built on site and the former maltings were closed. Since 2014 they have effectively housed a second distillery.

THE TUN ROOM ▶

Glen Ord's eight Oregon pine washbacks have now been doubled. Long fermentations play an important role in developing the fruity/floral character of the spirit (orange peel, nectarines, perfume), which is filled out by sandalwood and flaked almonds during maturation.

OLD PULTENEY

Fresh and maritime, with almond oil and fruit

Huddart Street, Wick, Highlands and Islands KW1 5BA
www.oldpulteney.com

The Old Pulteney Distillery was built in 1826 as part of the development of the northern port of Wick by the British Fisheries Society. The man put in charge of the scheme was one Sir William Pulteney, who in turn appointed a 33-year-old engineer, Thomas Telford, as Surveyor General. Telford chose a site on the south side of the river Wick for his harbour and new town. By 1807, the river had been bridged and four years later the harbour was completed, attracting fishing boats from all over the British Isles. Although Pulteney died before the work was completed, the new village was named after him. Today, Thomas Telford is recognized as 'the Father of Civil Engineering'; had it not been for his patron, this honour would not have been his.

The builder of the distillery was a local man, James Henderson of Stemster, who had held a licence to distil at the nearby village of Latheron since 1821 (although according to Alfred Barnard he had been distilling for nearly 30 years, presumably illegally). His descendants owned the distillery until 1920, trading as James Henderson & Company. Subsequent to this Pulteney passed through several ownerships – including

the Distillers Company Ltd (DCL), who closed it in 1930, then sold it on to 'Bertie' Cumming, owner of Balblair, in 1951. It is said that they had offered it for sale during the 1940s for £500, on condition that it be decommissioned. Today it is owned by Inver House Distillers, who bought it in 1987.

Pulteney Distillery has several unusual features – not least its stills (*see above*) – and one that has not changed since its foundation is its water source. Both process and cooling water comes from the Loch of Hempriggs, via the longest lade or millstream in Europe: 3½ miles long, with a drop of only 3.8 metres, it was designed by Thomas Telford to supply water to all Pulteneytown. It is still in perfect working order and until the 1920s, the water drove a waterwheel which supplied all the power to the distillery.

In his book *The Whiskies of Scotland* (1967), Professor R J S McDowell declared: 'It is to me quite surprising that such a good whisky could be made in this grim windswept fishing town on the North Sea. Caithness is indeed a bare county and needs a good whisky to warm it up...' My sentiments entirely.

COMPLEX STILLS

Pulteney's stills are peculiar. The wash-still (*foreground, left*) has the largest boil-ball in the industry and a flat top (rather than the usual swan neck). The smaller boil-ball spirit still (*background, left*) takes the shape of a 'smugglers' kettle'; it has a right-angled lyne arm which then bends straight down to a purifier that is no longer used. Both stills have worm tubs. The resulting spirit is heavy, although it becomes lighter during maturation.

NEW STILLS
The wash- and spirit stills are made of
copper and distillation takes up to four hours.
The longer exposure to copper leads to a
smoother spirit.

WOLFBURN

Light and fragrant spirit

Henderson Park, Thurso, Caithness KW14 7XW
www.wolfburn.com

Spirits first began to flow from the most northerly distillery on the Scottish mainland on 25 January (St. Andrew's Day) 2013, making Wolfburn the newest distillery to join the long tradition. So there is no mature whisky as yet, hence my tasting note ('light and fragrant') refers only to the spirit. The distillery buildings stand near the ancient town of Thurso on the edge of the Flow Country – 990,000 acres of blanket peat and wetlands. It is the largest such area in Europe and is currently a 'tentative' UNESCO World Heritage Site on account of the wildlife it supports. The site is close to that of a former distillery of the same name which operated between 1821 and 1852 (and maybe sporadically into the 1870s).

All that remains of the original distillery today is a pile of stones. However, as the founders of the new distillery point out, the cold, clear water of the Wolf Burn, which supplied both process and cooling water, still flows as it always has – and 'if the Wolf Burn was still there, we reckoned the whisky could be too.'

The image adopted by the founders as the symbol of their distillery is interesting. It was drawn by a 16th-century physician and naturalist, Konrad Gesner and appears in his work *The History of Four-footed Beasts and Serpents*. At that time wolves were common in the far north of Scotland and did much damage to cattle, the key commodity in the Highland economy. They were also said to dig up new-made graves and eat the corpses. In 1577, King James VI made it compulsory in Sutherland to organize wolf hunts at least three times a year. There are reports that wolves survived in Scotland up until the 18th century and even a suggestion that a wolf was seen in 1888. Interestingly, the wolf depicted by Dr Gesner is a 'sea wolf' – a semi-mythical creature related to the inland variety. According to legend, the sea wolf 'liveth both on land and sea' and Gesner's woodcut is thought to depict it walking on water. A sea wolf (in person or in an image) is also said to bring good luck to those who see it.

Wolfburn plan to release the first single malt in 2016, in a batch of 500–600 bottles. They aim to produce around 70,000 bottles per year in the future.

▲ DUNNET HEAD AND BAY

The village of Dunnet sits on the northeast corner of Dunnet Bay, while the Wolfburn Distillery's site lies to the west of the bay. Backed by significant dunes and home to many thousands of wading birds, Dunnet Bay is a vast expanse of sand. Visitors to the Seadrift Visitor Centre on the bay's northern end have access to a great viewing point, binoculars, a telescope and reference books to help identify the wildlife.

DUNNET BAY ▶

Dunnet Head lighthouse was built in 1832 and marks the most northerly point of the Scottish mainland, being just over 2 miles north of John O'Groats. Its 92 metres cliffs sit above the Pentland Firth, which separates Caithness from the Orkney Islands.

Moray Firth

Fraserburgh

Elgin

Nairn

River Spey

Knockdhu

River Deveron

Inverness

Glendronach

Glen Garioch

River Don

Grampian Mountains

River Dee

Aberdeen

Balmoral Castle

Royal Lochnagar

Fettercairn

Montrose

EAST HIGHLANDS

The East Highland region lay above the original Highland Line as it was drawn by the Wash Act of 1784, but in the 1797 amendment it was placed almost entirely below it. The countryside is rich and fertile: Angus' berry fields, the rich red earth of the Mearns and the rolling hills of the Garioch, Aberdeenshire, Buchan and Banff. Castles and towers abound.

A total of 76 distilleries are known to have existed here, falling naturally into two groups, roughly corresponding to the old county boundaries of Forfarshire and Aberdeenshire. Only one distillery, Fettercairn, has survived in what was once Forfarshire, while nine now exist in Aberdeenshire. The City of Aberdeen itself was once home to a dozen distilleries – none of which has survived – and also to the Chivas Brothers' shop, creators of the Chivas Regal blend.

Eastern malts tend to be medium to full-bodied, smooth and sweetish, but with the typically dry Highland finish. They are malty and often slightly smoky; sometimes fudge- or toffee-like, with notes of citrus, ginger and spice. They benefit from maturation in expensive sherry-wood casks for an enhanced flavour.

FETTERCAIRN

Butterscotch, nuts and spice

Distillery Road, Fettercairn, Laurencekirk AB30 1YB
www.whyteandmackay.com

Fettercairn Distillery was built by Sir Alexander Ramsay in 1824 and originally formed part of the Fasque Estate. He established it in a former corn mill at the foot of the Grampian Mountains, close to the market town of Fettercairn. This area is the western edge of the fertile Mearns country and the distillery is surrounded by extensive arable land stretching for miles; it is 'good corn country', as the poet Robert Burns would have said.

Like so many other distilleries, the site was formerly used by smugglers, about whom 'many a racy tale' was told, according to whisky historian Alfred Barnard. Barnard goes on to remind us that Kenneth III, King of Scots, was murdered on the Fasque Estate in 970 CE, while he was a guest of Fenella, daughter of the Earl of Angus. Her son had been executed on the king's order, so his stay was perhaps ill-considered. Tradition has it that Fenella showed the king into an opulent chamber containing a statue with lethal capabilities. She invited the king to take a golden apple from the statue's hand. As he did so, arrows shot out of the statue and killed him.

Six years after Sir Alexander Ramsay built the distillery, he sold it along with the entire estate to Sir John Gladstone, father of the British Prime Minister, William Gladstone. James Durie was appointed manager and he later acquired the distillery, passing it on to his son David Durie when he died in 1884. Just three years later the distillery was largely destroyed by a ferocious fire and a new company – The Fettercairn Distillery Company –with Gladstone's grandson John at the helm, began a rebuilding project. When liquidation threatened in 1912, the Gladstones bought out all their partners, but this was not enough to secure the distillery's future; the whisky slump of the early 1920s led to its closure in 1926.

In 1939, the distillery was bought and reopened by Associated Scottish Distillers, a subsidiary of The National Distillers of America, who doubled capacity. After 1971, it changed hands several times before becoming part of Whyte & Mackay, Glasgow distillers and blenders, which itself was bought by the Philippines-based brandy producer, Emperador, in 2014.

ICONIC HORSE

The Helladic horse, Greek symbol of alcoholic 'nectar', is the logo
for Whyte & Mackay, owners of Fettercairn Distillery. Until 2014, the
company was part of the United Breweries Group, which was founded
by a Scotsman, Thomas Leishman, in 1857; now it is owned by the
Philippines-based spirits firm, Emperador Distillers Inc.

BURN WATER

The process water used for mashing comes
from the Dronac Burn, which flows through
the distillery and provided the inspiration
for the distillery name. Barnard writes that
'although [the water is] tinged with a golden
brown, it is perfectly bright and clear'.

GLENDRONACH

Rich dried fruits

Forgue By Huntly AB54 6DB
www.glendronachdistillery.co.uk

Redcurrant jelly is good for the belly.
Ginger and nuts are good for the guts.
But the wine of Glendronach is good
for the stomach.

So ran the old saw, or poem and it was no doubt put about by James Allardice, who founded Glendronach Distillery in 1825 under the patronage of his landlord, the 4th Duke of Gordon. The Duke was so impressed by Mr Allardice that he introduced him to London society, among whom he apparently established something of a reputation for his 'Guid Glendronach'. This, at least, is one explanation of the malt's early success. However, another tale speaks of a much more lowly, but fascinating, start.

The story goes that one day in 1826, Allardice travelled to Edinburgh, keen to introduce his whisky to the pubs and people of the city. He travelled there with a large barrel and a flagon and set about selling the malt to local publicans. However, they explained that they already had all the stock they needed for the season, so no orders were placed. Wandering disconsolately back down the Canongate to his hotel, Allardice was accosted by two 'ladies of the night', who pressed him to take them for a drink. 'Ah

hae my aine guid Glendronach,' he told them and took them back to his hotel room for a drink. By all accounts they drank rather too much, but the next day they returned for more. Having given up on sales, Allardice gave them the remains of the flagon. Within 24 hours Canongate was full of inebriated women and the entire neighbourhood was talking about it. Everyone was determined to sample the malt and asked for it in the pubs by name. Allardice quickly sold out.

Allardice was also a welcome guest at Gordon Castle, home of the 4th Duke of Gordon, who paved the way for Allardice's malt in several ways. In addition to leasing him land and promoting his drink to friends, he steered the Excise Act of 1823 through Parliament, thereby laying the foundations of the modern Scotch whisky industry.

Relations between the two men were not always cordial. On one occasion, having had a little too much to drink, Allardice was judged to be 'over-effusive' in his praise of the Duchess of Gordon's piano playing. The following morning, the Duke informed him coldly that the Duchess was not amused, to which the bold Allardice replied: 'Well, Your

Grace, it was just the trash of Glenlivet you gave me yesterday after dinner that did not agree wi'me. If it had been my ain guid Glendronach, I would not hae been ony the warr.' A cask of Glendronach was ordered immediately and the friendship re-established.

In 1837 the distillery suffered a disastrous fire and required an extensive rebuild. Just over a decade later, it was sold to Walter Scott, former manager of Teaninich Distillery. He owned and managed the operation until his death in 1887, when it was bought by Captain Charles Grant, youngest son of William Grant of Glenfiddich, for £9,000. Some 73 years later, his son sold the distillery to William Teacher & Sons, who expanded it to four stills – its present capacity.

Glendronach was mothballed by its owners Allied Distillers in 1996, but it reopened in 2002. The floor maltings ceased, but, unusually, the stills remained direct-fired by coal until September 2005, when Allied Distillers was taken over by Pernod Ricard and Glendronach was put in the hands of Chivas Brothers. In July 2008, Glendronach was sold to Billy Walker, owner of Benriach Distillery and one of the best-regarded distillers in the business. He has created what is accurately described on the distillery's website as a 'renaissance'.

THE COURTYARD ▼

The original distillery buildings create an enclosed cobbled courtyard, often replete with rooks. It is said that as long as these birds remain, Glendronach will be lucky. One of the distillery's whiskies is named 'Parliament' after the collective noun for a group of rooks.

200 YEARS OF TRADITION ▶

Glendronach is proudly traditional. Its mash tun (above) is one of the few remaining old-fashioned, cast-iron rake-and-plough models and its nine washbacks (below) are made from Douglas fir.

GLEN GARIOCH

Toffee, ginger and spice

Distillery Road, Inverurie AB51 0ES
www.glengarioch.com

The Garioch – pronounced 'Geery' – is a richly fertile valley, some 250 acres in extent, bounded on every side by rolling hills. Glen Garioch Distillery stands on its eastern border, in the quaint market town of Oldmeldrum, around 18 miles northwest of Aberdeen. It is the most easterly distillery in Scotland and one of its oldest, dating back to 1797. Very much a family business at its inception, its founder, John Manson, was just 27 when he built the distillery; he was joined four years later by his 19-year-old brother, Alexander and was later succeeded by his own son, named John after his father.

John II's son, Sir Patrick Manson, was something of a medical genius – he was the first person to demonstrate conclusively the connection between mosquitoes and diseases such as elephantiasis and to postulate the origins of malaria, earning for himself the sobriquet 'Mosquito Manson'. He is widely recognized as 'the father of tropical medicine'.

The Manson family relinquished ownership in the 1880s and the distillery passed through several hands, including the Distillers Company Ltd, who mothballed it in 1968 on account of 'chronic water shortages and limited production potential.' They sold it to the Glasgow whisky broker, Stanley P Morrison, who also owned Bowmore Distillery on Islay. Morrison decided to do something about the water shortage and brought in a water diviner known as 'the Waater Mannie', or more formally, as Neil Mutch of Foggieloan. The Waater Mannie discovered a spring in a neighbouring field, which proved to be such a good water source that production rose to ten times its previous level.

Morrison extended the stills from two to four and also rebuilt large parts of the distillery. In 1973 the distillery released its first single malt and in 1995 it produced the last Glen Garioch to be made with smoked barley from its own maltings. The distillery had long used peat from nearby New Pitsligo Moss to give a light smokiness to the spirit, but it closed the maltings in the early 1990s and today the malt comes from independent maltsters and is unpeated. The current owners, Morrison Bowmore Distillers, now part of Suntory of Japan, release all of the whisky made at Glen Garioch as single malt.

ABERDEEN SPIRIT

The charming old buildings of Glen Garioch Distillery epitomize the sound, no-nonsense approach of the people of Aberdeenshire. The oldest parts date from the 1700s, but most of the buildings were constructed during the 1880s, when extensive improvements were undertaken by the then owner, J G Thomson & Co, blenders in Leith.

BEHIND THE SCENES
There is much that is charming and traditional about Glen Garioch and the distillery held to the old ways until the mid-1990s – direct-fired stills, on-site maltings – but the old-fashioned buildings now house modern equipment: a full-Lauter stainless steel mash tun with a peaked canopy, six stainless steel washbacks and a singe pair of stills, fired indirectly by steam-heated coils and pans.

KNOCKDHU

Fresh, citric and floral

Main Road, Knock, Huntly AB54 7LJ
www.ancnoc.com

Knockdhu Distillery lies in farmland near the village of Knock, in the shadow of the great Knock Hill, the 'black hill' or *Knockdhu* that gives the distillery its name. It owes its existence to landowner John Morrison, who bought the Knock Estate from the Duke of Fife in 1892 and discovered a spring of crystal clear water on the southern slopes of Knock Hill. He sent samples to a firm of analysts that happened to be retained by the Distillers Company Ltd (DCL). The results caught DCL's interest and they bought the property from Morrison to build a distillery.

Knockdhu therefore became the first malt whisky distillery commissioned by the DCL. This powerful company was originally an amalgamation of Scotland's six leading grain distillers, who between them controlled 75 per cent of grain spirit production in 1877. They banded together with the official aim of 'avoiding undue competition' and 'regulating supply to demand'; in other words, to avoid over-production and control prices.

The success of blended Scotch during the 1890s persuaded the directors of the DCL to commence malt whisky production at Knockdhu. Apart from the remarkable water supply, the site benefited from lying alongside fine barley country and an inexhaustible supply of peat. In addition, the Great North of Scotland Railway line between Elgin and Aberdeen ran adjacent to the site, providing a ready means of transport.

Constructed in 1894 from locally quarried grey granite, the *Banffshire Journal* described the distillery as 'commodious and complete, with every possible arrangement having been introduced with the object of saving manual labour'. During the 1920s, its manager wrote: 'In our business hours everything goes smoothly and pleasantly… The varied duties make time pass so quickly that Saturdays succeed each other with amazing rapidity.' Unfortunately the Great Depression was looming on the horizon and Knockdhu was mothballed between 1931 and 1933. It closed again between 1940 and 1945, owing to wartime restrictions on the supply of barley and during this period was occupied by a unit of the Indian Army, who were billeted in the malt barns along with their horses and mules.

Modernized in the 1960s and converted from direct firing to internal

UNIQUE WORM TUBS

Knockdhu is one of only a few distilleries to retain traditional worm tubs for condensing the alcohol vapour. Those at Knockdhu are unique because they allow both the spirit and wash worm to share the same cooling tub.

heating by steam coils in 1972, the distillery operated cheerfully until 1983, when it was one of the many casualties of the economic downturn and drastically reduced production. Five years later it was sold to Inver House Distillers, who released Knockdhu's single malt for the first time in 1990. Fearing confusion with Knockando Distillery, in 1993 they changed the name of the single malt from 'Knockdhu' to 'An Cnoc' – the local people's colloquial name for Knock Hill.

In recent years Inver House has introduced an eco-friendly way of stripping copper residues from the spent lees (the residue left in the spirit still after distillation), by pumping it into a wetland area containing 17 species of copper-neutralizing plants. This means there is no need to transport the spent lees to a waste-treatment facility, saving 8–10 tanker trips each week.

131

◄ A MODEL DISTILLERY

Substantially built of sparkling pale-grey granite of local origin, Knockdhu was described by a visitor in 1925 as being 'remarkably well-kept, both inside and out... A handsome avenue leads up to the main buildings and a small orchard of apple, cherry and plum trees, planted near the maltings, lends a charming natural touch to the severe buildings. In the interior almost every corner is spick and span. A powerful electric light plant lights the whole of the premises.'

GRIST FOR THE MILL ►

In common with other malt distilleries in Scotland, Knockdhu uses a very simple device to measure the ratio of flour, husk and grits in the ground malt – the 'grist' from the mill. This is a box fitted with two trays, each of which has a sieve for a base. The sieve on the upper tray has a coarser mesh than the lower one. The top tray is filled with a sample of grist, then the box is vigorously shaken so that only the husk is held back. The finer particles (the grits) drop through to the first level and the very fine particles (the flour) fall right through to the base of the box. Then the mill-man measures the amount of each: what he is looking for is 10 per cent flour, 20 per cent husk and 70 per cent grits.

◄ KNOCKDHU STILL HOUSE

Knockdhu has one pair of stills, but they are substantial. Based on the 'boil-ball' design, they are unusually tall, have strangely flattened pots and are capable of producing 1.9 million litres of spirit each year. The style of the spirit is estery, fruity/floral, with notes of lemon and it is given additional body by the worm tubs.

A FARM DISTILLERY

Royal Lochnagar is set comfortably into the
landscape of Royal Deeside, with the pine-
covered hills of Balmoral Estate rising behind
it. Groves of ancient Scots pines mark out
places that were once sacred to the early
peoples who inhabited this part of Scotland,
the Kingdom of the Northern Picts.

ROYAL LOCHNAGAR

Grassy, with light toffee and sandalwood

Crathie, Ballater AB35 5TB
www.discovering-distilleries.com

The 1823 Excise Act encouraged illicit distillers to take out licenses and switch to legal production, but those smugglers who took advantage of it were often resented by their former colleagues. One hotbed of smuggling in the early 19th century was Remote Upper Deeside, which became home to Royal Lochnagar Distillery. When its founder, James Robertson of Crathie, built a small distillery on the north bank of the River Dee, it was promptly burned down by smugglers. So he opened another in 1826, also on the north bank of the river, but in 1841 this also mysteriously burned down.

Robertson had named this second distillery Lochnagar, after the prominent mountain which dominates the view to the south. Its magnificence was recorded by the poet Lord Byron, who was descended from the Scottish kings of the 15th century through his mother, Catherine Gordon of Gight. In one of his best-known poems, *Lachin y Gair* (1807), Byron describes the mountain's appeal over anything England has to offer:

England! thy beauties are
tame and domestic
To one who has roved o'er
the mountains afar:
Oh for the crags that are
wild and majestic,
The steep frowning glories
of the dark Loch na Garr.

Given its previous history, it took a brave man to consider building another distillery in the area and yet in 1845 a man named John Begg did just that. He founded 'New' Lochnagar on the Abergeldie Estate, to the south of the river. Three years later, Queen Victoria and Prince Albert took up residence for the first time at Balmoral Castle, half a mile away. Knowing Prince Albert's interest in 'all things mechanical,' Begg immediately invited him to inspect his 'works.' Somewhat cheekily, he suggested that the royal visitors would need to arrive before 6pm, or they would miss seeing the distillery in action. Surprisingly, the royal family, including the three oldest children, came walking down the road to the distillery the very next day.

After he had shown them round, Mr Begg asked the Prince 'whether he would like to taste the spirit in its matured state, as we had cleared some that day from bond, which I thought was very fine. HRH having agreed to this, I called for bottle and glasses (which had been previously in readiness) and, presenting one glass to Her Majesty, she tasted it, followed by the rest of the family. 'HRH the Prince of Wales was going to carry his glass quickly to his mouth. I checked him, saying it was very strong and so he did not take but a very small drop of it.' The Prince of Wales was then aged only seven; his brother Alfred, who also tasted the whisky, was four! Within days John Begg had received a Royal Warrant of Appointment as 'Distiller to Her Majesty' and was granted permission to describe his distillery as 'Royal Lochnagar'.

Surrounded by the dark woods of the Balmoral estate, the distillery is the smallest and one of the most charming in Diageo's portfolio (it joined the DCL, Diageo's antecedent, in 1916). The present buildings, which date from the late 19th century, are built of solid Aberdeenshire granite and still have the character of a small farm distillery. Until 1963, a steam engine and waterwheels powered the distillery plant. Diageo has named the distillery its 'Malts Brand Home' and they use it to showcase all their malt whiskies, run training courses and entertain VIPs.

▲ LOCHNAGAR

The mountain of Lochnagar, part of the Caledonian Alps, dominates the landscape behind Royal Lochnagar Distillery. In the early mornings, slightly eerie mists roll off the mountains into the glen and around the distillery.

◄ A ROYAL DISTILLERY

The distillery was awarded a Royal Warrant in 1848 by Queen Victoria, following the royal family's visit to the new distillery. As a result it became 'Royal Lochnagar'. The distillery supplies Balmoral Castle with an exclusive malt named Balmoral Whisky, for sale in the castle gift shop.

Ben Nevis

Fort William

Loch Linnhe

Grampian Mountains

Mull

Oban

Firth of Lorn

Colonsay

Jura

Glasgow ■ River Clyde

Islay

Bute

Kintyre

Arran

Springbank

Firth of Clyde

WEST HIGHLANDS

There have been surprisingly few licensed distilleries in the West Highlands, apart from those at Campbeltown on the Kintyre peninsula. So it is somewhat surprising that early travellers recorded the widespread availability of whisky. This must have been illicit, as private distilling was banned in 1781. Policing such a remote and diverse territory was almost impossible and magistrates, who were also landowners, tended to favour the smugglers. Distilling was small-scale because the barley crops in the region suffered from high rainfall and poor land, so most of the whisky was drunk locally, although some was smuggled to the large cattle markets at Lairg and Falkirk. Significantly, most of the known distilleries in the West Highlands were within easy reach of Glasgow by sea.

Transport has long been an issue here. The two surviving distilleries on the west coast today, excluding those in Campbeltown, are both at rail-heads: Oban and Fort William. Campbeltown is a special case, because it has always had access to local coal and barley grown on the Kintyre peninsula, together with sea shipping. Today the town has three distilleries.

BEN NEVIS

Butterscotch, nuts and spice

Lochy Bridge, Fort William PH33 6TJ
www.bennevisdistillery.com

The founder of Ben Nevis Distillery was 'Long John' Macdonald, so named for his unusual height: he was 1.93 metres tall. Long John was chosen by the local landowners in Lochaber to head up their distillery on account of his charisma and probity, although he was only 27 years old. This was in 1825, but he maintained an air of unimpeachable rectitude throughout his life. The impression he made was well summed-up by an English tourist who met him in 1856, the last year of Macdonald's life: 'When a man goes to Caprera he, as a matter of course, brings a letter of introduction to Garibaldi. When I went to Fort William I, equally as a matter of course, brought a letter of introduction to Long John... I presented my letter and was received with the hospitality and courteous grace so characteristic of the Old Gael.'

Long John's distillery was small, producing around 900 litres of spirit a week, but it had a reputation as big as his own. It was sited in the garrison town of Fort William, at the foot of Ben Nevis and used the pure spring waters from Buchan's Well, Scotland's highest spring. Its quality was widely acclaimed and in 1848 a cask had even been accepted by

Queen Victoria, to be broached for the Prince of Wales' 21st birthday in 1863.

After the 'Old Gael's' death, the business passed to his son, Donald Peter Macdonald and although not as flamboyant a character as his father, it was Donald Peter who really laid the foundations of the distillery's success. By 1864 the distillery was producing 13,500 litres a week and in 1878 he built another, bigger distillery in the town, which he named 'Nevis'. The two distilleries sat close to one another, near the mouth of the River Ness and shared a pier and steamers.

On Peter's death, the distilleries passed to his sons and on their deaths they were bought by Joseph ('Joe') Hobbs, a colourful character who made a fortune in Canada from various enterprises, including running Scotch whisky into the United States during Prohibition. Hobbs introduced a patent still, concrete mash tuns and maturation in beer barrels. During the 1980s the distilleries belonged to Whitbread PLC, but in 1989 ownership passed to the famed Nikka Whisky Distilling Company of Japan (itself part of Asahi Breweries Ltd).

The
BEN NEVIS DISTILLERY
and
Visitor Centre

IN THE SHADOW OF BEN NEVIS
The distillery takes its name from Ben Nevis, the highest mountain in Britain. Its process and cooling water come from Coire Leis, 'the Leeward Corrie' and Coire na'Ciste, 'the Corrie of the Coffin', two lochans that sit at 915 metres near the summit of Ben Nevis itself.

▲ OLD INVERLOCHY CASTLE

Built in the 13th century by John 'The Black' Comyn, Lord of Badenoch and Lochaber, the castle was the backdrop for two important battles: the first in 1306, the second in 1645, when the royalist Marquess of Montrose defeated the covenanting army led by the Marquess of Argyll.

INVERLOCHY CASTLE HOTEL ▶

Soon after World War II, Joseph Hobbs bought Inverlochy Castle, a Victorian building not to be confused with the 13th-century castle nearby (*above*). His original intention was to convert it into a distillery, then he decided to restore it as his own country residence. On his death in 1964 his daughter converted it into a luxurious country house hotel.

▲ OBAN BAY
Even before the town was founded, Oban Bay was used as a safe haven by local fishermen. The bay is commanded by the prominent ruin of the 13th-century Dunollie Castle, seat of the MacDougall Lords of Lorne, which sits on an eminence to the south of the bay.

OLD AND NEW ▶
Oban is a traditional distillery, with an old-fashioned cast-iron 'rake-and-plough' mash tun and worm tubs on both its stills, but behind the scenes are modern pumps and piping that need constant monitoring and adjustments to ensure the quality of the make.

OBAN

Fresh fruits with maritime notes

Stafford Street, Oban PA34 5NH
www.discovering-distilleries.com

The port of Oban is the centre for importing and exporting from the Western Isles and the town grew up around its distillery during the late 18th and 19th centuries. The distillery was originally built as a brewery by brothers Robert, John and Hugh Stevenson, local 'worthies' who also had interests in slate quarrying, house-building and shipbuilding in the district. It is squashed between the high street and a steep cliff, close to the town centre. In 1890, when the cliff was being blasted to make room for a new warehouse, a cave was discovered, containing human bones and tools dating from around 4000 BCE.

Distilling historian Alfred Barnard reported in 1887 that the Oban Distillery was 'a quaint old-fashioned work and dates back prior to the existence of the town, having been built in the year 1794… by the family of Stevenson, the founders of the town of Oban, which previous to their advent was only a small fishing village.' The distillery remained in the Stevenson family until 1866, by which time Oban had become 'the great rendezvous for tourists in the West Highlands,' according to Black's *Picturesque Tourist of*

Scotland. Steamships sailed twice a week to and from Glasgow and Fort William and carried visitors to Staffa, Iona and Skye. Ships also carried Oban whisky to Glasgow and brought in coals and grain.

In 1880, with the arrival of the railway, Oban began to expand substantially and became the main hub of travel on the West Coast. A new owner 'modernized' the distillery at this time and converted the Stevensons' house – which stands at the entrance to a courtyard, adjacent to the still house – into offices. As a precaution, he retained a small peephole in the sitting room through which he could observe operations in the still house.

In 1898, Oban Distillery was bought by a consortium of distillers and blenders led by Alexander Edward of Sanquhar Estate, near Forres, a leading figure in the whisky industry of the day and a noted philanthropist. In 1930 Mr Edward sold the Oban Distillery Company to Scottish Malt Distillers, the production division of the Distillers Company Ltd (DCL). This later became a part of Diageo, who today promote Oban single malt as part of their Classic Malts range.

SPRINGBANK

A subtle complexity

9 Bolgam Street, Campbeltown, Argyll, PA28 6HZ
www.springbankwhisky.com

Arguably the most archaic of Scotland's malt whisky distilleries, Springbank enjoys cult status among connoisseurs for the quality of its old-fashioned style of whisky. It is also remarkable in being the only distillery established in the 19th century that is still owned by members of the founding family today. It was founded in 1828 by William Reid; by 1837 he was in financial difficulties and ownership passed to his in-laws, John and William Mitchell. It is believed that their father, Archibald, may have been distilling illegally on the same site before William Reid went into business. Two more of Archibald's sons, Hugh and Archibald Jr, had founded Riechlachan Distillery on the same street as Springbank and there were three others besides. The street quickly became known as 'Distillers' Row.'

Springbank sits in the fishing port of Campbeltown, which Alfred Barnard justifiably named 'The Whisky City.' When he visited the town in the 1880s, it was home to 21 distilleries, employing over 250 men. But this was the high point of the town's fortunes; during the late 1880s and '90s, blenders were looking for lighter, more fragrant malts – such as those found on Speyside – rather than the heavy and variable Campbeltown malts. Many of the town's distilleries closed before World War I and a further 17 were shut down during the 1920s, leaving just three: Springbank, Glen Scotia and Riechlachan.

John and William Mitchell quarrelled and in 1872 William left to join his other brothers at Riechlachan, while John brought his son Alexander into the business, which became and remains, J & A Mitchell. The company's present chairman is Mr Hedley Wright – John Mitchell's great-great-grandson.

Springbank has long been highly regarded and is eagerly collected today. As long ago as 1974, the *Daily Mail* reported that a hotelier in the Scottish Borders was displaying a bottle of 50-year-old Springbank at 10p a viewing. The paper noted that 'he paid £29 for it – the wholesale value of the whisky… If the liquid gold was up for sale (which it isn't), he would put a price tag of £20 on a fifth-of-a-gill measure.' How times have changed: a bottle of 50-year-old (from the same batch of 36 bottles) was sold at auction in 2001 for £3,800 and today would probably achieve four times that amount.

SPRINGBANK'S MALTING FLOOR

When whisky historian Alfred Barnard visited Springbank in 1885, there were four malting floors. Now the dried grain is stored in bins outside the main buildings, before it is brought up to 48 per cent moisture level in a steep and spread out on the malting floor for just over five days. The grain is turned every eight hours using a traditional malt mower that has already given around 100 years' service. The great distilleries of Campbeltown provided employment for many craftsmen and artisans, such as coopers (barrel and cask makers), peat-cutters and farmers, as well as directly employing still-workers and maltsters.

The production regime at Springbank is one of its many peculiarities: it has three stills and employs a complex, near-triple distillation to make three different styles of whisky: Springbank (lightly peated, 2.5 times distilled); Longrow (heavily peated, twice distilled); and Hazelburn (unpeated, three times distilled). Longrow and Hazelburn take their names from former distilleries in Campbeltown, as does Glengyle, a new distillery built by J & A Mitchell in 2004.

The distillery malts all its requirement in its own floor maltings, using locally cut peat and at least a proportion of locally grown barley. It is the only distillery to meet its entire requirement, apart from Glen Ord, which has a large drum maltings next door. It is also one of only two distilleries to manage its entire process – from malting to bottling – on the same premises. J & A Mitchell bought the independent bottler, Cadenhead's, in 1969, at around the same time it bought its neighbour, Longrow Distillery. In 1997, the company released the triple-distilled Hazelburn for the first time – and in 2009 it released the 12-year-old version. The name recalls one of Campbeltown's greatest old distilleries; in the late 1880s it was the largest, most productive distillery and was famed for its triple-distilled spirit.

Until July 2013, Springbank was managed by one of the most senior figures in the whisky trade, Frank McHardy, who had served the industry for 50 years. Frank began his career as a shift worker at Invergordon Distillery, then worked in several distilleries, including managing Springbank from 1977 to 1986, before becoming Master Distiller at Bushmills in County Antrim, Ireland, for ten years. He then returned to Campbeltown as Director of Production for Springbank and Glengyle Distilleries. He did not leave the industry completely, however, as he runs Springbank's annual Whisky School.

▲ BOTTLING LINE

Springbank is one of only four distilleries to bottle on site; the others being Bruichladdich, Kilchoman and Glenfiddich. It is the only distillery to malt 100 per cent of its requirement on site and to fire its wash-still directly by oil flame and indirectly by internal steam coils. It is also unique in using a worm tub on one of its two spirit stills (the other has a condenser) and in making three different whiskies in the same three stills.

◄ CHOOSING A CASK

Containers for whisky are generically called 'casks', because they come in different shapes and sizes. The most common are American Standard Barrels (ASBs), which hold about 200 litres and have already been used for 2–3 years for maturing bourbon or rye whiskey. Springbank also uses remade hogsheads (5 barrels are cannibalized to make 3 hogsheads, of around 250 litres capacity) and three other containers each holding 500 litres: sherry butts (seasoned with oloroso sherry), puncheons and port pipes.

Moray Firth

Glen Moray

Elgin

BenRiach

Benromach

River Lossie

Aultmore

Nairn

Strathisla

River Findhorn

Glen Grant

Macallan

Glenrothes

Aberlour

Cardhu

Tamdhu

The Balvenie

Knockando

Glenfiddich

Cragganmore

Glenfarclas

River Spey

The Glenlivet

Grampian Mountains

SPEYSIDE

Speyside is the heartland of whisky production: today, nearly two-thirds of the malt whisky distilleries in Scotland are found in the region. In Aeneas Macdonald's classic book *Whisky*, published in 1930, he wrote: 'It would be no true – or, at least, no very discerning – lover of whisky who could enter this almost sacred zone without awe.' His words still ring true and yet, until the 1823 Excise Act there were only two licensed distilleries in the region. The whisky was virtually all illicit, mainly because the district was so remote that farmers could distil illegally with impunity.

It was said that there were 200 illicit stills in Glenlivet in 1815, but only two licensed distilleries: Strathisla and Dalvey (now closed). When the 1823 Excise Act reduced distillation duties for whisky, 16 farmer-distillers took the opportunity to become legitimate and nine of these are still in operation today. In the mid-1880s, production exploded; 23 distilleries were built during the 'whisky boom.'

Blenders could not get enough of the sweet, fragrant, sophisticated malts of Speyside. A further 10 distilleries were built here between 1958 and 1974. Speysides fall into three broad categories – light, medium and full-bodied – and are generally unpeated. They have great finesse and

ABERLOUR

Sweet, with fresh fruits and spice

Banffshire AB38 9PJ
www.aberlour.com

Until relatively recently it was believed that the water used to make whisky dictated its flavour; as a result, the water source took on almost mystical significance. Aberlour can boast having a sacred well on site, dedicated to St Drostan, a follower of St Columba, who visited Speyside around 600 CE and later founded a monastery at Deer, Aberdeenshire, where the famous 10th-century gospel *The Book of Deer* was later written.

St Drostan reputedly used the well for baptizing wild Highlanders; so far as I'm aware it was never used for making whisky. Aberlour's process water comes from springs and its cooling water from the Lour Burn. *Lour* is Gaelic for 'chattering' and Aberlour means 'the mouth of the chattering burn.' Until the 1890s the distillery was entirely powered by water from the burn, which used to supply a meal mill and a sawmill.

In 1825, a distillery was established by the laird of Aberlour, James Gordon, who lived in Aberlour House nearby. At about the same time, he gave George Smith of Glenlivet, who had just taken out a license for his small distillery at Drumin, a pair of hair-trigger pistols to protect himself against jealous smugglers (*see* Royal Lochnagar, *pp. 134–7*). In 1833 the lease was taken over by John and James Grant, in partnership with two brothers named Walker. When the lease ended in 1840, the Grants moved to Rothes and founded Glen Grant Distillery, while the Walkers went to Linkwood Distillery.

Aberlour Distillery as it stands today dates from about 1880, when it was rebuilt by a local businessman, James Fleming, using granite from the same quarry that provided stone for Thomas Telford's famous bridge at Craigellachie, 2½ miles away. Fleming sold it to the Greenock blenders R Thorne & Sons in 1892; in 1898 it was largely destroyed by fire and again rebuilt.

The distillery's recent history dates from 1945 when it was acquired by the small Ayrshire blending house, S Campbell & Son, who expanded it to four stills, then sold both the company and the distillery to Pernod Ricard, the famous French spirits company, in 1974. Pernod Ricard began to promote Aberlour as a single malt, particularly in France, where it is the market leader. Today it is among the ten bestselling single malts in the world.

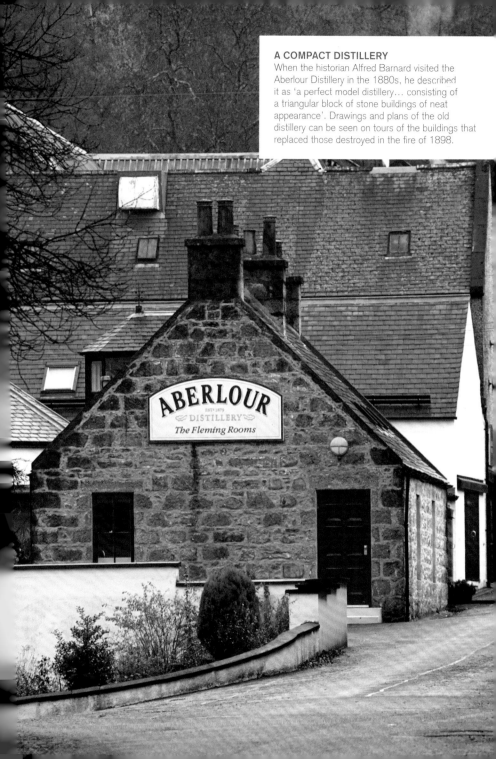

When the historian Alfred Barnard visited the Aberlour Distillery in the 1880s, he described it as 'a perfect model distillery… consisting of a triangular block of stone buildings of neat appearance'. Drawings and plans of the old distillery can be seen on tours of the buildings that replaced those destroyed in the fire of 1898.

▲ BONDED WAREHOUSE

Aberlour has six bonded warehouses on site, with the capacity to hold 27,000 casks, about half of which are ex-sherry butts. They used to enjoy the sound of music, because Ian Mitchell, who worked at the distillery for 48 years, was a keen piper and was accustomed to play his pipes in the warehouses, believing that the sound waves helped the whisky to mature. His grandfather, father and brother also worked at Aberlour.

▲ **THE WHINSTONE TOWERS**

In the 1930s the Aberlour Distillery built a pair of towers, known as the Whinstone Towers, to purify its waste water. Inside the towers, the water passed through many layers of wood and minerals to purify it, before it was released into the burn. Since the introduction of tighter environmental controls, this purification system has become redundant, but the towers are testament to Aberlour's longstanding commitment to the environment.

◄ **THE SCIENCE OF WHISKY**

Scotch whisky is made from a 'mash' of malted barley and water. Three waters or 'extractions' are used in the mashing process and each is heated to a particular temperature for a set length of time. The temperature of the water increases with each extraction, before the warm wort that is produced at the end of the process are cooled to 20°C to stop the maltose from decomposing and killing off the yeast.

AULTMORE

Sweet and fresh-fruity

Main Road, Knock, Huntly AB54 7LJ
www.ancnoc.com

Aultmore Distillery derives its name from the Gaelic *allt mhor*, meaning 'big river', because it stands near the River Isla, itself a tributary of the mighty River Tay. The area in which it sits is lightly populated, rolling farmland known as 'the Foggie Moss' and the actual hamlet of Aultmore only came about as a result of the building of the distillery, in 1896.

The Moss was formerly a popular haunt of illicit distillers and the spirits made here were taken to local towns where they were in great demand with publicans and innkeepers. As late as 1934 an elderly local remembered a 'small still' being worked by one Jane Milne and the *DCL Gazette* of that year notes that four bothies (temporary buildings that housed illicit stills) were 'visible in the burn and gullies where an ample supply of water could be obtained.'

Although the excellence of the water supply played a part in the choice of the distillery site, the main reason was its proximity to the Great North of Scotland Railway (GNSR), to which the distillery was connected by a spur to the Keith-Buckie line. The distillery's founder was Alexander Edward of Forres, who had inherited Benrinnes Distillery from his father and then built Craigellachie

Distillery. He was the shooting tenant over the Foggie Moss site for some years, renting from its owner, the Duke of Fife, but in 1896 he purchased the land outright, together with a couple of farms. He then sold on the land to the Aultmore Distillery Company, which he owned.

Work began on the site immediately. Alexander Edward was 32 years old at the time and *The Banffshire Herald* remarked: 'Mr Edward's success in having amassed an independent fortune before he was barely entered in his thirties is regarded as a perfect marvel. He is not contented to make his pile by the thousand, but by his potent tact and skill can accomplish this by the tens of thousands.'

The distillery was designed by Charles Cree Doig of Elgin, the leading distillery architect of the day and it was in production by May 1897. It was a good time to found a whisky distillery, because it was the height of the Victorian 'whisky boom', which was driven by the popularity of blended Scotch. Aultmore was immediately successful – indeed it was ranked 'Top Class' by blenders. The following year, extensive alterations and improvements were announced and the distillery's capacity was doubled to 450,000 litres a year.

THE FOGGIE MOSS
The distillery stands on the edge of an area of wild country known as the Foggie Moss, a remote and spooky place whose numerous water springs and abundant peat deposits made it a haunt of illicit distillers in the 19th century.

As a result of its success, Aultmore was very difficult to find as a single malt, although it continued to be a much sought-after secret dram of the locals, who would ask at the local inn for 'a nip of the Buckie Road'. It quickly became even more scarce, because Edward suffered serious losses following the crash of Pattison's of Leith and Aultmore was sold to John Dewar & Sons in 1923, becoming part of the Distillers Company Ltd (DCL) when Dewar's joined the larger entity two years later.

The floor maltings were closed in 1968 and Aultmore was rebuilt. However, its malt was not bottled by its owners until 1996 and even then, only in small quantities. Two years later, Diageo (the successor to DCL) sold Dewar's and four distilleries, including Aultmore, to Bacardi. Happily, in 2014 the new owners released expressions at 12, 21 and 25 years old.

No.2
WASH STILL
Contents 22970 Litres

◀ **AULTMORE STILL HOUSE**

Aultmore has two pairs of stills. These are the two plain, onion-shaped wash-stills, with their long, tapering lyne arms leading to shell-and-tube condensers, making for an elegant, light-bodied spirit that is very popular with blenders.

▲ **STEAM ENGINE**

A 10-horse-power Abernethy steam engine was installed in 1898 to supplement the original source of power, a waterwheel driven by a lade (or flume) from the distillery dam. All the distillery's machinery was interconnected to allow it to be powered by either the steam engine or the waterwheel. The wheel gave service for almost three-quarters of a century and is preserved at the distillery today.

161

THE BALVENIE

Full-bodied, dried fruits, honeycomb

Duff Town, Moray AB55 4BB
www.thebalvenie.com

William Grant opened Glenfiddich Distillery (*see pp. 186–91*) in 1886, just as the first 'whisky boom' was developing. In order to protect his amenity, he bought 12 acres of adjacent land in March 1890, including 'Balvenie New House' and Balvenie Mains, a 1,000-acre farm. In 1892 he built The Balvenie Distillery in the grounds of Balvenie New House.

The New House was actually a neo-Classical mansion, commissioned in 1722 by William Duff, later 1st Earl of Fife, from the prominent architect James Gibbs. It is said that Duff built it for 'a beautiful countess', who had been gifted a greyhound by a local admirer. The dog turned out to be rabid, and its bite killed the countess, after which the house was abandoned by its owner. When William Grant bought the semi-derelict building from his descendant, Alexander Duff, it had been lived in for only eight years and been derelict for eighty.

The new distillery went into production on 1st May 1893, and was originally named Glen Gordon, and the old mansion house was converted into a maltings. The following year, another pair of stills was added, and today it has five wash-stills and six spirit stills in two still houses, with a capacity of 6.4 million litres per annum. More than 245,000 nine-litre cases of Balvenie were sold globally in 2013 – an increase of 90 per cent over the past 10 years – and the brand stands at number eight in world volume sales.

The distillery grows its own barley on Balvenie Mains farm (albeit only a tiny amount), has its own floor maltings (producing about 10 per cent of its requirement), its own coopers and coppersmiths, and its own bottling facility. (It also runs apprenticeships to train its own coopers.) The malt made on site is lightly peated with peat from New Pitsligo Moss, near Pennan on the Moray Firth, while the bought-in malt is unpeated.

Ownership of The Balvenie has remained within the Grant family. Its single malt was first bottled in the 1920s, then in the famous triangular bottle used for Grant's 'Standfast' blend, followed by Balvenie Founder's Reserve in a striking Champagne-style bottle in 1982. In 2014 two expressions of 50-year-old single malt were released, priced at £25,000 per bottle.

THE MALTINGS
The Balvenie is one of only nine distilleries that still malts its own barley on site, in traditional floor maltings that incorporate the pagoda-topped kilns invented by Charles Cree Doig of Elgin, the leading distillery architect of his day. Some of the barley coming into the maltings grows on Balvenie Mains farm, also owned by William Grant & Sons.

▲ THE CONVAL HILLS

The Balvenie and its sister distillery, Glenfiddich, both draw their process water from the pure Robbie Dhu springs in the Conval Hills. Balvenie distillery itself sits on the lower slopes of the Convals, which look spectacular when covered in heather blossom during the summer.

THE SPIRIT ▶

The 'boil-ball' design of pot still is also known as the 'Balvenie ball', which suggests that the design was first employed at The Balvenie Distillery. The stills are maintained by the distillery's coppersmith, who has looked after them for 60 years.

BENRIACH

Apples and green bananas with vanilla cream

By Elgin, Morayshire, IV30 8SJ
www.benriachdistillery.co.uk

Benriach – or BenRiach, as its current owners prefer – was built by John Duff in 1897 and designed by Charles Cree Doig of Elgin, the famous distillery architect. However, it did not follow the E-shaped design that Doig usually favoured; its buildings ran in lines on either side of the railway track that ran to the distillery from Longmore junction. Though its transportation links were good, the distillery occupied a somewhat isolated stretch of rural land below the Grampian Mountains, close to the River Lossie.

Duff was a publican and former manager of Glendronach Distillery. In 1876 he went on to build the Glenlossie Distillery in partnership with a couple of local businessmen, before emigrating to South Africa in 1888 with his family. There he attempted to establish a distillery in Gauteng Province in the Transvaal, where gold had recently been discovered. However, for reasons unknown, Duff's distillery failed and he moved on to the USA, where he founded yet another unsuccessful distillery.

Undaunted, Duff returned to Scotland in 1892 and was employed as distillery manager at Bon Accord Distillery, Aberdeen. The following year he commissioned Longmorn Distillery, then BenRiach – so close to Longmorn that at the time it was named Longmorn No.2. But by 1899, the unlucky John Duff was in financial difficulties again and he sold BenRiach to his partners at Longmorn, who kept only the maltings in operation. BenRiach was to remain closed until 1965, when it was rebuilt and reopened by Glenlivet Distillers Ltd. Over the next 30 years it changed ownership several times and in 2002 was again mothballed, before being bought by a small, independent consortium in 2004 led by Billy Walker, a distillery chemist who has been called 'the smartest man in whisky'.

BENRIACH FROM LONGMORN

BenRiach Distillery was originally named
'Longmorn No.2' and for many years supplied
its sister distillery with malt. Until 1980 the
two were connected by a private railway,
goods being drawn latterly by a 'puggie'
diesel locomotive, which is today preserved
at Aviemore.

▲ PURIFYING THE SPIRIT

The spout on the spirit still is directed manually from one bowl to the other. The early runnings of spirit, called foreshots, are high strength, pungent and impure: they are directed to the foreshots and feints receiver for redistillation. Then the spout is moved over to the spirit receiver to save 'the heart of the run', which will be filled into casks. After this the spout is again moved so the last fraction – the feints – join the foreshots for redistillation.

▲ BENRIACH MALTINGS

When BenRiach was owned by Seagram, who acquired it when they took over DCL in 1978, the maltings at BenRiach were still in operation. However, they were decommissioned in 1998. Walker was determined to reopen them and his consortium received the first malt to be used for distilling in September 2013. It turned out to be substantially more expensive than commercial malt, but it is still hoped that around 10 per cent of 'homemade' malt may be viable.

SHARED WAREHOUSING ▶

In days gone by, blenders sent their casks to distilleries to be filled and each company painted their cask heads a different colour so they could be easily identified. In those days, Longmore and BenRiach also warehoused their spirits together and their casks were identified by colour and warehouse number. Past owner Chivas (who sold the distillery to Walker's consortium) still owns some of the warehoused whisky, though BenRiach owns the majority of the 28,000 or so casks.

BENROMACH

Fresh fruit, light cereal, good body

Invererne Road, Forres, Morayshire IV36 3EB
www.benromach.com

The name Alexander Edward crops up repeatedly in the story of Speyside distilling during the late 19th century. Edward inherited Benrinnes Distillery from his father, then built Craigellachie Distillery (in partnership with Peter Mackie, *see p. 48*) and Aultmore Distillery (*see pp. 158–9*). He also bought Oban Distillery (*see pp. 144–5*) and finally, in 1898, he supported Duncan Macallum and F W (Walter) Brickmann in establishing Benromach Distillery on the edge of his own estate, Sanquhar, outside Forres, near the mouth of the River Findhorn.

Edward and his partners employed the leading distillery architect of the day, Charles Cree Doig of Elgin, to design their new building. Doig, today best known as the inventor of the pagoda-roof ventilating system, built a distillery with high-pitched gables and narrow, mullioned windows in the Scots vernacular style of the 17th century. Alas, disaster struck even before the distillery went into production. Pattison's of Leith, one of the largest blending firms in the country, went into liquidation. F W Brickmann, who was himself a spirits broker in Leith, was closely associated with Pattison's and his firm was suspended in 1899, with

liabilities exceeding £70,000 (equivalent to around £3 million today). In 1901, criminal proceedings were raised against the Pattison brothers, Robert and Walter, for 'fraudulent floatation, other frauds and embezzlement'. Robert was sent to prison for 18 months and Walter for eight months. Confidence in the Scotch whisky industry, which had been so strong for a decade, was shattered.

Benromach finally commenced production in 1909, but just two years later was sold to Harvey McNair & Co, London. This firm owned the distillery for eight years, spanning the period of World War I, during which the distillery was closed. Times were hard; the distillery changed hands several times during the first half of the 20th century and there were long periods of closure. In 1953 it was bought by the Distillers Company Ltd (DCL), along with several other distilleries, but they closed it in 1983 and removed all the plant.

Then, in 1993, Benromach was bought by Gordon & MacPhail (G&M) of Elgin. This company had been founded as a general grocer, wine and spirits merchant in 1895 and in 1896 it took on a new partner, John Urquhart, to assist with selecting and

buying casks of whisky. He was joined by his son, George, who was to take the unprecedented step of launching a range of single malts. When he did this, in 1956, malt whisky was more or less unknown beyond the Highlands of Scotland. So George looked abroad: during the 1960s and '70s he promoted his malts in Italy and France and his efforts paid off. Italy rapidly became the first country to embrace malt whisky (well before the UK and USA) and France is now the third-largest consumer of Scotch in the world. It had long been George Urquhart's ambition to own a distillery and he realized this dream in 1993 when G&M bought Benromach. It took five years to re-equip the distillery and put it into production and George died just four years later. Today, G&M is owned and managed by his descendants.

1 PEATING THE MALT

Benromach's own maltings closed in 1968 and today its malt is supplied by local independent maltsters. It is peated to around 10 parts per million (ppm) phenols – sometimes heavier, sometimes lighter. Benromach's Peat Smoke whisky, for instance, has a considerably higher level, at 67ppm.

2 WOODEN WASHBACKS

When Gordon & MacPhail bought the distillery in 1993, there was nothing left on site except a single receiver tank, so everything is new. However, there is much that is traditional at Benromach, including the wooden washbacks, made from Scottish larch. During the 1920s, the distillery uniquely had a wooden mash tun.

A CONSTANT SPIRIT ▶

Details of the last cask to be filled at the 'old' Benromach Distillery, on 24 March 1983, are recorded on a white-washed wall. G&M replaced all the equipment, installing smaller stills than had been used in the distillery's previous incarnations (it is the smallest operating distillery on Speyside). They performed test runs to establish the desired flavour of the spirit. These were then compared with samples from the previous distillery. Astonishingly, the old samples were identical to the spirit now being made, yet the only constant features between the two were the water source and the location – neither of which should make any difference to spirit character.

CARDHU

Fresh fruits, floral and bright

Knockando, Aberlour, Banffshire AB38 7RY
www.discovering-distilleries.com

Cardhu, or Cardow as it was spelled until 1981, was among the first distilleries on Speyside to be licensed. Its owner was John Cumming, who had been distilling illegally on his small farm since at least 1810, when he became the tenant. He was caught and fined several times before eventually gaining a licence in 1824.

Cumming was ably assisted by his formidable wife, Helen. In the early 19th century the location was remote (Barnard decribes it as 'a wild and desolate district') and there were consequently very few inns to accommodate visiting excisemen. So Helen would innocently welcome them as lodgers at the farm. Once the excisemen were safely sitting at the supper-table, Helen would hoist a red flag over the barn to alert her neighbours of their dangerous presence.

In truth, Helen was responsible for the distilling operation at Cardow Farm, which she oversaw for more than 60 years. After John's death in 1846, she was assisted by her son Lewis. Her whisky was carried by horse and cart to Burghead on the Moray Firth to be shipped to Leith, until the Strathspey Railway line opened in the 1860s.

Lewis died in 1872, leaving a wife, Elizabeth and three small children.

Elizabeth proved to be as formidable as her mother-in-law, whom she began to assist. A year before Helen's death, aged 98, Elizabeth obtained the feu (a Scottish form of lease) of a piece of ground close to the old distillery and built 'an entirely new distillery, on the most approved plan.' Alfred Barnard visited Cardow just after the new buildings had been erected and described the new distillery as 'a handsome pile,' especially in comparison to the old buildings, which he disparagingly remarked were 'of the most straggling and primitive description and although water-power existed, a great part of the work was done by manual labour. It is wonderful how long this state of things existed, considering the successful business that was carried on for so many years.'

Interestingly, Barnard also commented that the spirit from the new distillery 'had been submitted to competent judges, who pronounced it to be similar in character to that made at the old distillery, which is of the thickest and richest description and admirably adapted to blending purposes.' This is curious, as today's spirit is light and floral-fruity in character.

CARDHU DISTILLERY

This is a view of Cardhu Distillery from across the River Spey and shows its proximity to what was once wild open moorland, now forestry. The distillery's elevated location afforded some protection from the attention of officials in the days when the Cummings were illicit distillers.

175

Charles Mackinlay & Co, in Leith, were the agents for selling the new-make spirit to blenders and it commanded a high price. In 1893, Elizabeth Cumming was able to sell Cardhu to one of her leading customers, John Walker & Sons of Kilmarnock, under the condition that her son, John Fleetwood Cumming, should join the Walker board. (John's son, Ronald Cumming, would rise to become chairman of DCL.)

The Cardhu make was now in the hands of John Walker & Sons. By 1923, this company was led by Sir Alexander Walker, the grandson of John Walker and he took a keen interest in the quality of the spirit made at Cardhu. Like many others, he subscribed to the widely held belief that it was unlucky to interfere with the spiders in the tun room, as they were thought beneficial to fermentation. On his orders they were therefore a protected species and when a new brewer at Cardhu unwittingly cleaned and repainted the room, he was furious. According to the company archivist,

Brian Spiller, 'Sir Alexander's anger, when he discovered this act of impiety, was long remembered.'

Notwithstanding this, Walker's quickly expanded and modernized the plant and by 1924 a dynamo provided electric power for the entire site, including the workers' cottages. A trade journal remarked at that time: 'It is hardly necessary to add that electric light in country cottages is extremely rare and the privilege is greatly appreciated.' Following the amalgamation of Walker, Buchanan-Dewar and DCL in 1925, Cardhu became part of the larger entity, although John Walker & Sons retained the license to distil and Cardhu continues to constitute a major part of the Johnnie Walker blend. In the 1960s Cardhu underwent extensive modernization and expansion, when the still house, mash house and tun room were all rebuilt and a further pair of stills was installed. In 1997, the DCL and Cardhu were bought by Diageo, who still own the distillery today.

A MASTER'S NOTES
Among the treasures kept at Cardhu are Alexander Walker's blending books. Dr Jim Beveridge, Walker's current master blender, has studied them exhaustively and sometimes feels that he is being overseen and guided by the spirit of Sir Alex.

THE HOME OF JOHNNIE WALKER
The visitor centre at Cardhu, which opened in 1998, houses a large collection of Walker memorabilia: portraits of the Walker brothers, old photographs, and both old and new bottles of Johnnie Walker. It is situated in the old maltings and provides excellent hospitality to invited guests.

CRAGGANMORE

Green bananas, leather, dried fruits

Ballindalloch AB37 9AB
www.discovering-distilleries.com

John Smith, the founder of Cragganmore Distillery in 1869, is said to have been the leading distiller of his day. He had managed Macallan Distillery and the new Glenlivet Distillery at Minmore (its present location) in the 1850s, before going south to run Wishaw Distillery in Lanarkshire and finally returning to Speyside in 1865 to manage Glenfarclas Distillery, on land owned by Sir George Macpherson-Grant of Ballindalloch.

The Macpherson-Grant family had owned Ballindalloch Castle and estate (including the land Smith wanted) for over 500 years and they continue to do so today. They granted Smith the lease and, in 1869, agreed to lease him a further piece of land on which stood Ayeon Farm, half a mile from Ballindalloch Station on the newly opened Speyside Railway line. This was to become the site of Cragganmore Distillery and it was the first on Speyside to take advantage of the railway. A private siding was laid down some 300 metres from the station to take distillery traffic. There was a massive increase in the number of Speyside distilleries during the 1890s, largely due to the railway.

The distillery and farm worked closely together, as was always the case in these days. The local newspaper, *The Elgin Courant*, noted the distillery's clever use of gravity to convey 'fattening drinks from the distillery, which pigs as well as oxen delight to imbibe and on which they become so stout as to be unseemly, but not less adapted for the London market.'

The agents for selling Smith's new-make spirit to blenders were James Watson & Co of Dundee, at the time a well-known firm and they had no difficulty in disposing of the entire output. In 1887 they arranged for the first 'whisky train' to leave Ballindalloch with a load of 73,000 litres.

John Smith died in 1886, aged 53 and for seven years the business was carried on by trustees, under the guidance of John's brother, who managed Parkmore Distillery in Dufftown, until John's son – Gordon Smith – was of an age to take over. George had learned distilling in South Africa and he soon decided that Cragganmore 'was too antiquated to do with further patching up... there was nothing for it but to build a practically new distillery.' Improvements were supervised by Charles Cree Doig, the leading distillery architect, but the plans were carefully laid out so that they did

A RAILWAY ENTHUSIAST
John Smith was a passionate railway enthusiast and lent his support to the construction of the Speyside Railway, which reached Ballindalloch in 1863. This made it possible to import coal, barley and casks and to export whisky. Unfortunately Mr Smith was such a large man that he could not enter through the railway coach door and had to travel in the guard's van! The station's nearby cattle court, embellished with the sign for Cragganmore station, was formerly a store for goods prior to their being loaded onto the train.

not affect the overall layout of the site. Nor did they interfere with the unusual design of the stills, which have flat tops rather than the usual 'swan necks'. This may increase reflux, which is formed by the spirit vapour condensing on the flat surface and then dripping down to be redistilled. However, any lightness of body that this might contribute is countered by the use of worm tubs. The result is a medium-bodied Speyside of unusual complexity (Cragganmore 12-year-old was chosen by United Distillers to represent Speyside when they launched their 'Classic Malts' selection in 1988).

Following Gordon Smith's death in 1912, Cragganmore was managed by his widow, Mary Jane. After a brief closure during World War I, when no barley could be spared for distilling,

she continued to build the business, installing electricity in 1919 via a petrol-driven generator on site. In 1923 she sold the distillery to the Glenlivet Distillery Company, whose parent company was White Horse Distillers Ltd and the Ballindalloch Estate. Its owners were Sir George Macpherson-Grant, Sir Peter Mackie (see Lagavulin, p. 48) and Alexander Edward (see Benromach, pp. 170–3). The White Horse Distillers shares were sold to the DCL in 1927 and the remainder went to them in 1968, making them sole owners of Cragganmore. Meanwhile, Sir George's descendants have turned elsewhere – they have restored a farm steading on the estate and created a second distillery, named Ballindalloch, which began production in the summer of 2014.

◀ **CRAGGANMORE DISTILLERY**

Not much has changed since *The Elgin Courant* described the distillery in 1870 as being laid out in an unenclosed square, with the maltings (now defunct) in the south block, the mash house and still house to the east, the spirit store and offices to the north and a warehouse to the west. In 1886, when Alfred Barnard visited the distillery, there were eight warehouses around the yard, which together could hold over a million litres.

▲ **THE SPEY VALLEY**

In 1886, Alfred Barnard visited Cragganmore and noted: 'We passed the palatial entrance to the castle of Ballindalloch and immediately afterwards crossed the bridge over the river Aven [sic], a fine stream, which takes rank as the third in Scotland for salmon fishing… Cragganmore is situated in the heart of a mountain district and close by the River Spey. The beauty of the Spey valley is enhanced by the contrast it offers to the wild and rugged scenery around it.'

GLENFARCLAS DISTILLERY

The hill behind the distillery buildings is Benrinnes, whose springs provided the water for the distillery in 1887, when the whisky historian Alfred Barnard visited. He wrote: 'Our journey to Glenfarclas was a longer affair than we expected, for what seems near in mountain scenery may be, after all, a long way off. Beautiful the prospect certainly was not; for without the soft magic of green hills, woodlands and the river meandering in the verdant meadow, no scene can deserve the qualification; nevertheless, if unlovely, all was strange, gigantic and sublime.'

GLENFARCLAS

Fruitcake and orange marmalade

Ballindalloch, Speyside, Banffshire AB37 9BD
www.glenfarclas.co.uk

Legend has it that distilling has been taking place in Glenfarclas, 'glen of the green grass', since the 18th century. A watercolour painting entitled 'Glenfarclass Disty', dated on the back '1791', depicts a substantial operation, yet there was no licensed distillery here at that time. The first name to appear on a licence to distil at Rechlerich Farm, site of Glenfarclas and part of the Ballindalloch Estate, was 'Robert Hay', who was the farm's tenant in 1836. When he died in 1865, his neighbour, John Grant of Blairfindy in Glenlivet, acquired the tenancy for the farm and bought the distillery; the latter cost him £512 (around £315,000 today). He was a very successful farmer – hence his interest in Rechlerich Farm – and initially he employed his cousin John Smith to run the distillery. When Smith left to build Cragganmore Distillery (*see pp. 178–81*), Grant's son George joined his father in partnership to run the farm and distillery. The Grants of Glenfarclas have owned and managed it ever since.

Successive generations of Grant men were all named John or George and this continues to the present day. George (I) died in 1890, leaving the licence to his widow until his boys, John and George (II), achieved their majority (at the time of his death, John was 17 and George was 16). John and George decided they could expand the business by going into partnership with Pattison, Elder & Company of Leith and the new company was called the Glenfarclas-Glenlivet Distillery Company. Pattison's became the agent for the new-make spirit and undertook to take 'the whole make of whisky.' The famous distillery architect, Charles Cree Doig, was employed to expand the distillery buildings.

Then came the crash (*see* Benromach, *pp. 170–3*). Pattison's

SINGLE MALT ▶
Apart from a tiny amount, the entire
Glenfarclas output was used for blending
until the late 1960s. It was the first company
to release a cask-strength expression,
Glenfarclas 105, in 1968. By 1967 4,000
cases of 10-year-old Glenfarclas were being
sold in the UK; today global sales are in
excess of 80,000 cases.

STEEL WASHBACKS ◢
Glenfarclas has 12 stainless steel washbacks
and ferments for 48 hours.

collapsed, owing Glenfarclas-Glenlivet over £27,000. The liquidators eventually paid back around £1,000, but the distillery and farm became mortgaged to the Caledonian Bank. By 1906 the brothers had managed to trade out of their difficulties and they resolved from then on to be independent. In 1912 the ebullient Sir Thomas Dewar, who used Glenfarclas in his Dewar's blends (*see* Aberfeldy, *pp.* 56–9) described Glenfarclas as 'The King of Whiskies and the Whisky of Kings... In its superiority it is something to drive the skeleton from the feast and paint landscapes in the brain of man.' Indeed, it was generally rated 'Top Class' by blenders, both then and now.

John (I) took early retirement and George (II) struggled on alone. In 1930, he managed to buy the freehold of the distillery and secure his rights to water and peat. He had married Jessie Stuart Scott in 1921 and they had two sons – George (III) and John (II). In 1947, George (II) incorporated a private limited company, J & G Grant Ltd, in which the shares were owned by his two sons. George (III) took over management of the distillery in 1946 and the demand for whisky began to increase rapidly, which was just as well, because when his father died in 1949, aged 72, the 'death duties' (taxes payable on death) amounted to the entire value of the company's share capital.

As a result George (III) received many offers to sell Glenfarclas, but he politely turned them all down. Capacity was doubled (to four stills) in 1959 and a new warehouse built. In 1968 orders slowed down as other distilleries opened, but this led to the laying down of more stock and accounts for the very old 'Family Casks' available now. George (III) was succeeded by his son John (III), whose own son, George (IV!), became a director in 2013.

GLENFIDDICH

Light, fresh and fruity

Dufftown, Banffshire, AB55 4DH
www.glenfiddich.com

Glenfiddich is far and away the bestselling single malt in the world, outselling its nearest rival by two to one. In 2013, sales topped one million cases (at 9 litres per case) for the first time. But in spite of its size and success, the owner of the brand – William Grant & Sons – is still controlled by direct descendants of its founder.

William Grant was the son of a tailor in Dufftown, who had served in the 92nd Regiment of Foot (also known as 'The Gordon Highlanders') during the Napoleonic Wars. The young William worked for a short time as a book-keeper in a local limeworks, before taking a similar job at Mortlach Distillery in 1866. It was the only distillery in Dufftown at the time and he worked there for 20 years, becoming its manager for the salary of £100 per year. This was at a time when the average

middle-class income was anything from £125 to £1,000, so his salary was by no means large and yet remarkably, he managed to save a portion each year. By 1886, with the help of his two oldest children, he was able to buy stills and other necessary distilling equipment from Elizabeth Cumming of Cardow (*see pp. 174–7*).

In September of the same year, he leased a site on Balvenie Mains Farm from its owner, the Duke of Fife. It was close to Old Balvenie Castle (*see pp. 162–5*), on the bank of the River Fiddich and supplied with excellent water from the Robbie Dhu springs on the slopes of the Conval Hills, close to the village of Glenfiddich. Assisted by his wife and eight of his nine children – aged between 23 and 10 – and just one stonemason, he began carting stones from the riverbed to build his distillery.

THE ORIGINAL BUILDING
The old malt kiln was the first part of the distillery to be built, the stones being carried up from the bed of the River Fiddich by William Grant's family. Today it forms part of the busy visitor centre (welcoming around 80,000 visitors a year) and houses the distillery's restaurant.

WILLIAM GRANT
The founder of Glenfiddich Distillery, William Grant, is shown here in the uniform of the local Volunteer Regiment, which he joined as a private and rose to be commissioned major. This was the highest rank to which a non-professional soldier could aspire to in peacetime. In his later years he was known simply as 'The Major'.

Within a year the distillery was built and producing single-malt whisky.

Fortunately for William Grant, soon after Glenfiddich went into production, a well-known firm of blenders in Aberdeen named William Williams & Company placed an order for 400 gallons (1,800 litres) a week. This constituted the entire output of the nascent distillery, giving it a sound base from which to expand production. By 1902 Glenfiddich was being bottled by the Grants in small quantities and within two years they had begun to sell some in Canada. This was the era of blended Scotch, however and the enterprising William Grant soon launched his own blend, named 'Standfast' (the motto of the Grant clan). By 1914 the firm had 63 agencies around the world.

Today, Glenfiddich has the largest number of pot stills in the world: 10 wash-stills and 18 spirit stills. Unusually, the stills are all direct-fired by gas burners; only one other distillery (*see* Glenfarclas, *pp. 182–5*) employs this traditional method for all its stills. Tradition counts for much at Glenfiddich.

THE GLENFIDDICH STAG
Glenfiddich translates from Gaelic as 'the valley of the deer' – hence the proud stag that decorates every bottle of Glenfiddich single malt. A life-size sculpture of the famous deer stands at the distillery.

1 A NOD TO TRADITION
The old buildings at Glenfiddich feature pagoda ventilators designed by Charles Cree Doig of Elgin, who invented this elegant way to draw hot air through the bed of damp green malt during the kilning process. The Glenfiddich kilns are not used today, but the distillery's newer buildings also feature Doig's pagodas as a salute to tradition.

2 THE COOPERAGE
Glenfiddich and its sister distillery, The Balvenie, pride themselves on doing everything 'in-house', including having their own coopers to assemble, repair and reconstruct casks. The casks themselves come from Kentucky, USA and Jerez, Spain and are mostly 'second-hand', meaning they have been seasoned with either bourbon or sherry. Unusually, Glenfiddich also uses a small number of fresh oak casks.

3 THE ROBBIE DHU SPRINGS
One of the reasons that William Grant chose the site was the availability of copious amounts of pure water. The Robbie Dhu ('Black Robbie') springs lie a short distance away in the Conval Hills; they bubble up from the ground and gradually become a stream. Soft and slightly acidic, this water is used at every stage of production.

4 A MAGNIFICENT GLEN
The landscape around Dufftown is at once majestic and domestic, combining gently rolling fields and woods against a backdrop of wild, heather-covered hills. As the old rhyme goes: 'Rome was built on seven hills, but Dufftown stands on seven stills'.

A DRAM BY THE BURN

The Glen Grant Burn (formerly known as
the Black Burn) tumbles down in a waterfall
beside a rustic summerhouse known as
the Dram Pavilion. It then flows through a
splendid Victorian woodland garden, laid out
by Major James Grant and restored in 1996.

GLEN GRANT

Sweet, with mown hay and green apples

Elgin Road, Rothes, Charlestown of Aberlour, Banffshire AB38 7BS
www.glengrant.com

When their lease at Aberlour expired in 1839 (*see pp.* 154–7), the brothers John and James Grant moved down the road to Rothes and built a new distillery. It was the first in the village and was said to be 'one of the most extensive distilleries in the North'. Goods were transported by road until the arrival of the Speyside Railway in 1858, and indeed this was a project in which James Grant (by now Provost of Elgin) was closely involved. One of the early train engines was named Glen Grant.

James Grant Jr, known as 'The Major' (not to be confused with the Major from Glenfiddich) succeeded his father in 1872, at the beginning of the whisky boom. Glen Grant was already being sold as a single malt, and was described as 'peculiarly adapted for family use [in] England, Scotland and the Colonies'. It was sold by the cask, but the distillery provided customers with its distinctive label, featuring two kilted Highlanders seated beside a cask, with the motto 'From the Heath Covered Mountains of Scotia I come'.

The Major lived the life of a Victorian laird in Glen Grant House, a baronial mansion that used to stand beside the distillery. He laid out a huge woodland garden that, in his day, required 15 gardeners to keep it neat. He was also a keen sportsman and his study in the visitor centre displays a number of trophies from hunting trips to Africa. On one trip to Matabeleland, he and a friend named Johan Colenbrander came across two abandoned, starving orphans. They decided to rescue them; one child went with Colenbrander back to Bulawayo, while the other returned to Scotland with the Major. The child was named Biawa (meaning 'by the wayside', in an allusion to where the boy was found) and was sent to the local school. Biawa later became the Major's valet and a well-respected figure in Rothes village. He lived in Glen Grant House until his death in 1972.

In 1931, the Major was succeeded in the business by his grandson, Douglas Mackessack, who expanded production and began to bottle Glen Grant as a 12-year-old, as well as the more usual 4-year-old, making it one of the earliest single-malt whiskies to be generally available. All malt whisky production ceased between 1942 and 1945, and for several years after that barley was rationed. But demand was at an all-time high, both at home and abroad; money was needed to expand capacity. Accordingly, in 1952, Glen Grant merged with George & J G Smith Ltd to form a limited company, and then in 1972 with Hill Thomson & Co, to become The Glenlivet Distillers Ltd.

Thanks to the entrepreneurial flair of the distillery's Italian agent, Armando Giovinetti, Glen Grant became the first single malt to take off in an export market. Giovinetti realized that a young expression would have most appeal (he was challenging grappa, the most popular Italian spirit), and he specified that the whisky should be five years old. He promoted this vigorously from the mid-1960s, and by 1977 was selling around 200,000 cases a year. Glen Grant remains Italy's favourite malt and is the sixth bestselling malt in the world.

In 1978, The Glenlivet Distillers Ltd was purchased by the Canadian drinks giant, The Seagram Company. In 2001, Pernod Ricard bought Seagram's Scotch whisky interests, and they were obliged by European monopolies regulations to sell Glen Grant. It was bought by Campari of Milan in 2006. Fortunately for continuity's sake, they appointed Dennis Malcolm – an employee at Glen Grant since 1961 – as distillery manager.

The heating of the stills at Glen Grant is curious. The original four stills were direct-fired by coal, the wash-stills having rummagers (sheets of copper chain mail, mechanically dragged around the base of the stills to prevent solid particles burning on and spoiling the flavour). These were driven by a waterwheel until 1979, making it the last one used in the industry. Two more stills were added in 1973, direct-fired by gas, and a further four in 1977. In 1979, all ten were converted to gas. However, this regime only lasted until 1983, when the wash-stills were reconverted to coal. All the stills were converted to indirect firing by steam-heated coils and pans in the late 1990s.

1 STILLS AND PURIFIERS
The Glen Grant label stresses that the whisky is 'distilled in tall slender stills' and uses purifiers. The unusually shaped stills and the purifiers were introduced by the Major in 1872; Alfred Barnard noted that they 'prevented anything but the purest steam from passing'.

2 BESPOKE BOTTLING LINE
Glen Grant installed its own bottling hall in 2013 – one of only a handful of distilleries to have the capacity to bottle on site. It cost £5 million and is capable of filling around 12,000 bottles an hour.

THE GLENLIVET

Sweet, with mown hay and green apples

4 Castleton of Blairfindy, Glenlivet, Ballindalloch AB37 9DB
www.theglenlivet.com

The first farmer-distiller on Speyside to take out a licence was George Smith. A trained joiner, Smith began farming and making illicit whisky in the early 1800s, at Upper Drimmin, Glenlivet. By 1816, he was producing it at the rate of 'about a hogshead a week' (250 litres). Smith was a tenant of the Duke of Gordon, who persuaded Parliament to alter the law so it was possible for small distillers to make good whisky and sell it at a reasonable profit. With the support of the Duke, Smith obtained a distillers' licence in 1824, a year after the law was changed.

However, Smith's decision to distil legally did not go down well with his former smuggling cronies, who were furious about the fact that he could openly go about the business of making whisky, while their efforts had to remain secret. They resolved to burn down his distillery, 'and him at the heart of it' (*see* Royal Lochnagar, *pp. 134–7*). For 10 years Smith carried a pair of hair-trigger pistols in his belt, a gift from the laird of Aberlour (*see* Aberlour, *pp. 154–7*), but as he said, 'I was then a robust young fellow and not given to be easily fleggit' (frightened).

The illicit whiskies made in the Glenlivet district had long had a high reputation: when King George IV visited Edinburgh in 1822, he is reputed to have 'drunk none other whisky' than Glenlivet. Four years later, the renowned Scottish poet James Hogg, also known as 'the Ettrick Shepherd', was quoted as saying: 'Gie me the real Glenlivet and I weel believe I could mak' drinking toddy oot o'sea-water. The human mind never tires o' Glenlivet.'

In the mid-1820s, George Smith appointed Andrew Usher as his agent in Edinburgh and in 1853 Usher released the first-ever branded Scotch whisky: Ushers Old Vatted Glenlivet. After 1860, this became a blend of three malts (including Glenlivet) and a grain whisky. By the 1880s, many other distilleries were adopting the name 'Glenlivet' because the term had become synonymous with what we now call Speyside. George Smith's son and successor, John Gordon Smith, therefore sought a court order to prevent the general use of the word and it was agreed that only Smith's whisky could call itself 'The Glenlivet'. All the other distillers could use the term only as a suffix, such as 'Aberlour-Glenlivet'.

A PLACE APART
In 1884, an exciseman stationed in Glenlivet captured the essence of the place, writing that it 'is a very remote part of the world... mountains surround us on all sides.'

THE GLENLIVET DISTILLERY
Glenlivet sits on the northeastern slopes of Carn Liath, at a height of 245 metres. The mountain itself provides a challenge for walkers and trekkers, many of whom make their way to the summit at 549 metres before descending for a 'wee dram' at the distillery's visitor centre.

In 1921 Captain Bill Smith Grant, who had served with the 1st Gordon Highlanders during World War I, inherited the distillery from his uncle. He managed to keep the distillery going during the whisky crisis of 1930–1, when many independent producers were obliged to join the Distillers Company Ltd (which owned a large number of Scottish distilleries) in closing for a season. They did this in an effort to influence the government into awarding the industry some fiscal relief, but this was not forthcoming. However, Prohibition in the USA – which had also been affecting trade – was repealed in 1933. Having stayed continuously open for business, Bill Smith Grant found himself in a strong position and he began to promote The Glenlivet as a single malt in the USA. By 1953, it accounted for half of all the Scotch malt sold there. Today it is still number one in this market and number two in the world.

▲ **THE MASH TUN**
The first thing you see on entering the new distillery is an enormous, gleaming mash tun, which may be the biggest in Scotland. It was installed during the distillery expansion of 2010.

THE STILL HOUSE ▶
In the 1880s the distillery had only one pair of stills, which produced 18,200 litres of spirit per year. After World War II, the distillery expanded to four stills (1964), then six (1974), then eight (1978). In 2010 a new distillery was built within thea existing site and a further eight stills added, increasing capacity to 10 million litres.

A BLEND OF OLD AND NEW
Like many distilleries, Glen Moray has been expanded over the years,
but when more stills are added, they are careful copies of the existing
stills: plain or onion-shaped with broad bases.

GLEN MORAY

Butterscotch, vanilla and barley water

Bruceland Road, Elgin, Morayshire IV30 1YE
www.glenmoray.com

Glen Moray Distillery stands on the western edge of the Royal Burgh of Elgin, on the former site of the town's gallows. In 1962, when excavations for a new warehouse were carried out at Gallow Crook Hill – where murderers were 'brint to the death' until the end of the 17th century – diggers unearthed seven skulls, one with a musket ball embedded in its jaw.

In the 18th and early 19th centuries there was a brewery on the site, which was famous for the quality of its water. Like so many others, the distillery was built in the late 1890s by a consortium of local businessmen, the Glen Moray-Glenlivet Distillery Company. Also like many others, it suffered from the downturn in the whisky industry after 1900 and closed in 1910. Ten years later it was bought by Macdonald & Muir (M&M), blenders in Leith and owners of Glenmorangie Distillery.

M&M brought the distillery back into production in 1923, reconstructed the site in 1958 and installed a second pair of stills in 1979, making use of the malt in their successful blends, notably Highland Queen. The single malt was first released in 1976, but only began to be promoted in the early 1990s.

Glen Moray was bought by the French spirits group La Martiniquaise in 2008 and has been dramatically expanded to provide fillings for their blended Scotch, Label 5. This is among the bestselling whiskies in France, which is the third-largest whisky market in the world, after India and the USA. Glen Moray itself is also very popular in France, where it is named Glen Turner. In 2012–13, the new owners installed a third pair of stills and plan to double the distillery's size, with a new mash tun, 12 new washbacks and six new stills.

▲ ANCIENT HISTORY

The old road into Elgin wanders right through the distillery grounds and is said to have been used by Macbeth himself (who was High Steward of Moray before becoming King of Scotland) when pursuing Duncan to his death in Elgin. The distillery itself is tucked in a hollow just beyond a residential area of the town.

THE RELIABLE PORTEUS ◥

Most distilleries in Scotland have mills made by the Porteus Company, who made the one shown here. They are incredibly heavy, reliable and simple to operate – and they last forever.In fact, so robust and long-lived are they that I believe the Porteus Company may actually put itself out of business!

MIXED WAREHOUSING ▶

Glen Moray has a mix of old, traditional dunnage and modern, palletized warehouses. The former are low, earth-floored and damp, with the casks stored three high. In the modern warehouses, the casks stand on end, six to a pallet, which is then lodged in place by fork-lift truck. They are drier and warmer than dunnage warehouses and mature their contents slightly differently.

GLENROTHES

Dried fruits, nuts and nougat

Rothes, Morayshire AB38 7AA
www.theglenrothes.com

Spirits first ran from the stills of Glenrothes on 28 December 1879. It was a ferociously stormy night, with winds gusting to 80 mph. Unknown to those at the distillery, that same gale brought down the railway bridge over the River Tay, which had been designed by engineer Sir Thomas Bouch to be 'indestructible'. It had been open only 19 months. As it collapsed, it pitched the night train from Edinburgh into the foaming Tay Estuary with a loss of all 72 passengers, the driver, fireman and ticket inspector.

This disaster was not the only inauspicious omen. By the late 1870s, Britain was involved in the worst economic crisis for over a century. The Long Depression hit the USA and Europe and in Scotland the effect was felt most strongly through the huge fall in grain prices, as cheaper grain from the New World flooded the market. Both the City of Glasgow Bank and the Caledonian Bank closed their doors. The partnership that had begun building Glenrothes Distillery in 1878 was dissolved and work ceased for some months, before production finally began in December 1879 under a new name, William Grant

& Co. This partnership consisted of two bankers – William Grant and Robert Dick – and a lawyer, John Cruickshank. In 1884 they renamed the company Glenrothes-Glenlivet.

The agents for the sale of Glenrothes new-make spirit were Robertson & Baxter, whisky brokers in Glasgow. W A Robertson, R&B's senior partner, suggested that the distillery merge with Bunnahabhain (*see pp. 38–41*) in 1887 to form the new Highland Distilleries Company (HDC). The two distilleries united and annual production at Glenrothes grew to 363,700 litres. HDC is still the owner today.

The make has long been ranked 'Top Class' by blenders. In 1896 it was included in the new Famous Grouse blend and around 30 years later it was to become a key filling for Cutty Sark. Recognizing the brand's potential early on, the owners extended the distillery to include four stills in 1896, using plans drawn up by Charles Cree Doig of Elgin, the leading distillery architect of the day. However, while work was proceeding, a fire devastated part of the site, even though the owners had installed Doig's

SURROUNDED BY SPIRITS

The still house at Glenrothes overlooks Rothes cemetery, which is of
considerable antiquity. Stories of ghosts abound: the wooded glen that
runs up the Rothes Burn behind the distillery is reputedly haunted by
the ghost of Lady Mary Leslie, daughter of the Earl of Rothes, who
was murdered here by the notorious Wolf of Badenoch (Alexander
Stewart, Earl of Buchan and son of the King of Scots). The distillery's
water source is The Lady Well where the same Lady Mary was done
to death.

COOPERS AT WORK

Glenrothes is unusual in having a cooperage on site, as was always the case in days gone by. Most distilleries today rely on centralized cooperages, like the Speyside Cooperage at Craigellachie, to check, repair and rejuvenate casks as required. Much of the Glenrothes spirit goes into Spanish oak ex-sherry butts; the rest goes into American oak, ex-bourbon hogsheads and barrels.

patented appliance for preventing explosions in the mill room. This was an ever-present risk in distilleries, owing to the presence of fine flour, which is easily ignited by a spark if there are any stones in the malt. Doig's invention seems to have been less than perfect – it also failed to avert another fire six years later!

Glenrothes was further enlarged in 1963 (to six stills) and 1983 (eight stills), then the still house was completely rebuilt in 1989, with ten stills. The stills themselves are large and tall, making for a light and complex style of spirit. The mature whisky is filled into uniquely shaped oval bottles, known affectionately in the trade as 'La Bombas' and the smaller, 10 cl bottles as 'Bombettes'. The top-of-the-range expressions of Glenrothes are poured into hand-blown crystal decanters of the same shape, but with a facetted surface and a stopper cork carved from the very cask the whisky has been drawn from.

PERSONALIZED BOTTLES

In 1987, Highland Distilleries licensed the Glenrothes brand to Berry Bros & Rudd, the long-established London wine and spirits merchants and owners of Cutty Sark (along with Highland). They released the first proprietary bottling that year, from 1975 stock – as a wine merchant, Berry Bros preferred to work in 'vintages' rather than age statements. Since 1994 the bottle labels have been inspired by the labels used for sample bottles.

FINE TASTING AREA

Knockando was one of the first distilleries to welcome visitors and provide facilities for entertaining them. A former store, which used to hold the 'dramming cask' from which the workforce were 'drammed' twice a day, was converted into a reception and party area.

KNOCKANDO

Sweet cereal and nuts

Aberlour, Moray AB38 7RT
www.springbankwhisky.com

Like many other Speyside distilleries, Knockando was built during the 1890s and designed by Charles Cree Doig of Elgin, this time for John Tytler Thompson, who was as ambitious as he was unlucky. The son of a hairdresser in Elgin, Thompson worked initially as a clerk, first for the railway and then for Miltonduff Distillery. At the same time he attended night classes in accountancy. On passing the exams, he opened a shop in Elgin High Street and began trading as a 'Spirit Broker & Scotch Whisky Merchant'. He then decided to open a distillery and the site he chose was a steep bank above a bend in the River Spey within Knockando Parish, fairly close to the Cardhu and Tamdhu distilleries. In 1899, *The Distillers' and Brewers' Magazine* noted that the new distillery was fitted 'with all the latest appliances for producing the greatest possible amount of work in the best manner and with the least labour.'

Alas for Mr Thompson, the whisky industry was about to go into severe recession. The collapse of Pattison's of Leith led the banks to withdraw their credit; as W H Ross, the managing director of DCL, noted: 'many firms were obliged to ask protection from their creditors, while others were hopelessly crippled in their future business.' Knockando closed in March 1900, just ten months after it had opened. It was sold to W & A Gilbey Ltd, the prosperous London wine and spirits merchants, three years later. John Thompson emigrated to Australia.

Gilbey's immediately expanded the distillery, installed a maltings, complete with the familiar pagoda-topped kiln and built a railway siding off the nearby Speyside. Most of the make from Knockando went into the company's Spey Royal blend. However, by the 1950s Gilbey's itself was in the doldrums and the once mighty company was overtaken by many of its competitors. In 1962 it merged with one of them, the distinguished and long-established firm of Justerini & Brooks, to form International Distillers & Vintners (IDV), now part of Diageo. Much of the make was diverted into the company's phenomenally successful blend, J&B Rare, but Knockando began to be offered as a single malt in 1976, stressing the year of distillation, rather than the age, in the manner of fine wine.

▲ KNOCKANDO DISTILLERY

The small huddle of buildings that make up the distillery sit on a high wooded bank between the villages of Knockando and Archiestown, in the majestic countryside of Morayshire. There are five on-site warehouses for the small amount of spirit (8 per cent) that is reserved for bottling as a single malt. The rest is shipped to Diageo's warehousing for use in its blended malts.

BY ROYAL APPOINTMENT ▶

Founded in 1749, Justerini & Brooks (J&B) received its first Royal Warrant from King George III in 1761 and this honour has been granted by every succeeding monarch, including HM Queen Elizabeth II.

MACALLAN

Rich with fruit and nuts

Charlestown of Aberlour AB38 9RX
www.themacallan.com

Macallan was one of the earliest distilleries on Speyside to be licensed, in 1824, but it is highly likely that there was a farm distillery here long before, since it was one of the few places where the Spey could be forded – and drovers are thirsty folk.

The founder of the licensed distillery was barley farmer Alexander Reid, who leased the land from the Earl of Seafield. By the mid-19th century the licence had passed on twice: the second time, in 1868, to James Stuart, who bought both the land and the business. When Alfred Barnard visited in the 1880s, he described it simply as 'an old fashioned establishment' with an output of 180,000 litres per year, most of which 'finds its way to the English market.'

In 1892 Stuart sold Macallan to Roderick Kemp, a master distiller and part-owner of Talisker Distillery on the Isle of Skye. He rebuilt and modernized the place, and it was under his ownership that the whisky won its high reputation among blenders. After his death in 1909, Macallan was owned and managed first by his trustees, then by his descendants, who formed Macallan-Glenlivet Ltd. The distillery was doubled in size (from six to 12 stills) in 1965 and the following year Macallan-Glenlivet went public. The money raised from this initial public offering, combined with the additional capacity, allowed the company to lay down stock for bottling as single malt, which was first released in the late 1970s. It was an immediate success in Italy, the USA and France, as well as the home market. Between 1981 and 1984, sales increased by 120 per cent and in 1987 a bottle of 60-year-old malt set a world record of £5,500 at auction.

In 1996 Highland Distilleries acquired a large stake in Macallan and pooled it with an equally large stake owned by Suntory. They mounted a successful hostile takeover bid and the company passed through a succession of amalgamating companies. Since 1999, it has been owned by the Edrington Group, who also own Highland Park (*see* *pp. 234–7*).

EASTER ELCHIES HOUSE
The large and rambling distillery grew up around the beautiful old mansion house of Easter Elchies, built in 1700 by Captain John Grant. In 1759 the house and estate were sold to the Earl of Seafield, who later leased land to Alexander Reid.

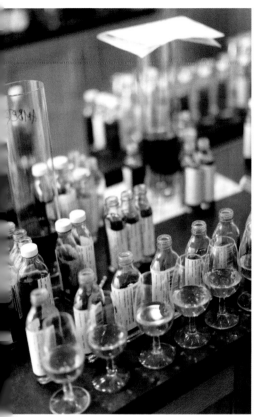

◄ **THE SMALLEST OF STILLS**

Macallan has the smallest spirit stills on Speyside and, unusually, its wash-stills are still directly heated by gas fires. In 1951, The Wine & Spirit Association noted that direct firing 'is a vital factor in developing the character and quality of Scotch Whisky, and bringing out its special peculiarities'. Small stills make for a more robust and oily spirit, which is especially suited to maturation in ex-sherry casks.

▲ **THE SEARCH FOR CONSISTENCY**

Macallan's chief Whisky Maker is Bob Dalgarno, and his assistant is Dhavali Gandhi. They have overall responsibility for the flavours in the entire Macallan range, and since no colouring agent is added to The Macallan, they have to make sure that, batch by batch, the liquid hue is constant by judicious cask selection.

FARMING ORIGINS

The layout of the distillery reflects its origin as a farm distillery.
Low stone buildings sit around a cobbled courtyard, adjacent to the
maltings, tun room and still house. The distillery was substantially
renovated by Seagram in 1965, who installed a second pair of stills
but were careful to retain the distillery's rustic charm.

STRATHISLA

Rich dried fruits and sandalwood

Seafield Avenue, Keith, Banffshire AB55 5BS
www.chivas.com

The original distillery on the Strathisla site was founded in 1786, making it one of the earliest surviving distilleries in Scotland and the oldest operating in the Highlands. At first it was named 'Milltown' and then 'Milton', but by 1825 the whisky itself was known locally as 'Strathisla'. The distillery duly followed suit and formally adopted this name in 1951.

Like Bowmore Distillery (*see pp. 32–3*), which was built around the same time, Milltown formed part of New Keith, a model village that was built in 1750 by the second Earl of Seafield to border the medieval village of Old Keith. The third Earl granted a lease to two local 'worthies', George Taylor ('flax-dresser, tailor and banker') and Alexander Milne, 'for the purposes of a distillery'. They installed a single still capable of holding 180 litres, which is tiny by today's standards and they had the legal right to distil 28 tons of malted barley a year.

In 1830 the distillery came into the hands of William Longmore, banker and grain merchant and the make became known as 'Longmore's Strathisla'. By the 1880s it had won a high reputation.

One diarist noted, 'wherever one travels, one finds that those who know what good whisky is speak in the most glowing and appreciative terms of the produce of Milton Distillery at Keith'. The company established by Mr Longmore operated the distillery until 1950. During its last four years it was controlled by a shady London financier named Jay Pomeroy, who siphoned off large amounts of Strathisla and disposed of it 'in a manner calculated not to attract any taxation liability', according to the judgment in the Court of Session. In fact, he sold it on the black market for huge profit, there being a chronic shortage of mature whisky at the time. Pomeroy was sent to prison; the company was wound up and bought at auction by Jimmy Barclay, one of the more colourful characters in the whisky industry of the day. Barclay immediately sold it to Seagram, the huge Canadian distiller, who had also acquired Chivas Brothers. They doubled the number of stills to four and built warehousing capable of holding 100 million casks of whisky. Strathisla became the flagship distillery for Chivas Regal, now owned by the French distiller, Pernod Ricard.

▲ TRADITIONAL WAREHOUSING

Whisky must be matured for a minimum of three years before it can be so named: when it comes off the still it is merely 'new-make spirit'. Strathisla stores its whisky in traditional warehouses – they have low ceilings, gravel floors and slate roofs and the casks are stored three high. This makes for ideal conditions: cool and damp, with a constant ambient temperature, whether it is summer or winter.

◄ VINTAGE STRATHISLA

The single malt known as Longmore's Strathisla was at one time stored in earthenware casks. Bottles of whisky from the distillery under the Longmore name occasionally come up for auction. In 2012 the auction house Bonhams sold a 'pre-1947' bottle for £2,814.

VICTORIAN WATERWHEEL

In the past most distilleries were powered by waterwheels. Strathisla's was installed in 1881 and it was used until 1965 to drive the 'rummagers' in the wash-stills. These were strips of copper links, not unlike chain-mail, which were dragged across the base of the still to prevent the sediment of the wash settling on the bottom of the still and burning. The water for distilling is – and always has been – drawn from the Broomhill Spring, which rises in the hill behind the distillery.

THE OLD OFFICE

Strathisla is among the prettiest distilleries in Scotland and the oldest working distillery in the Highlands. When the listed buildings were tastefully restored in 1995, visitor facilities were incorporated, including a re-creation of the old distillery office as it might have been in the 19th century.

TAMDHU

Rich with fruit and nuts

Knockando, Aberlour AB38 7RP
www.tamdhu.com

Tamdhu was one of three distilleries built in Knockando Parish during the 'whisky boom' of the 1890s, along with Knockando (*see pp. 208–11*) and Imperial (now closed). The two surviving distilleries sit close to a sweeping double bend of the River Spey, and virtually opposite each other.

The founder of Tamdhu was William Grant, who had been a partner in Macallan Distillery (*see pp. 212–15*), and had built Glenrothes Distillery (*see pp. 204–7*) in 1878. The latter was taken over by Highland Distilleries in 1887 and Grant was made a director of the company. The same year he was appointed agent of the Caledonian Bank in Elgin on a salary of £250 per annum, and then decided to finance his various activities with an overdraft that he had lent himself. The branch auditors raised this with head office on several occasions: by 1895, when the total branch deposits were £10,000, Grant's overdraft had reached £20,000! He was obliged to make over 1,500 shares in Highland to the bank in recompense.

Grant still managed to pull together a group of leading blenders to build Tamdhu, including Highland's sister company, Robertson & Baxter; John Walker & Sons; William Sanderson & Co; John Dewar & Sons; and Bulloch Lade & Co. The malt went into production in 1897, and the distillery was considered to be among the most modern in Scotland, with a capacity of around 900,000 litres per year. It also had access to its own substantial maltings. However, sadly, Grant quickly ran out of money again, and he was forced to sell Tamdhu to Highland Distilleries the following year.

Even this could not save the distillery from the effects of the Great Depression of the 1920s and it was closed from 1927 to 1947. Shortly after reopening, Saladin boxes were installed – a form of mechanical malting invented by Frenchman Charles Saladin in the 1890s. The distillery was among the first to install these boxes, and the last to stop using them – one was still in operation at Tamdhu until 2010.

Between 1972 and 1975 the distillery was partially rebuilt and greatly extended, and in 1976 the single malt was first released. In June 2011 Tamdhu was sold to an Edinburgh firm, Ian Macleod & Company, owners of Glengoyne Distillery and Macleod's Isle of Skye.

▲ STONE WAREHOUSES

Tamdhu has four traditional dunnage warehouses on site (two of which were built by the time of Alfred Barnard's visit in 1899) and one racked warehouse. The new owners plan to build a further six palletized warehouses. The different warehousing styles play a part in the rate and manner of the spirit's maturation.

◄ A RETURN TO TRADITION

One of the biggest changes made by the new owners has been to reposition Tamdhu as a sherried malt, maturing it in American and European oak sherry casks, both first- and second-fill.

Orkney Islands
Scapa
Highland Park
Thurso
Abhainn Dearg
Lewis
Outer Hebrides
NORTH SEA
Skye
Inverness
Talisker
Aberdeen
Inner Hebrides
Grampian Mountains
Tobermory
Dundee
Mull
River Clyde
Edinburgh
Glasgow
Jura
Islay
Isle of Arran

THE ISLANDS

Scotland has 790 islands and 99 of these are inhabited. Only six are home to distilleries: Arran, Jura, Mull, Skye, Lewis and Orkney. In days gone by, many more of the islands had small, illicit distilleries, which have long since disappeared.

The island climate is maritime and wet; the winds are fierce and farming is hard. Distilleries struggled to grow their own barley. Poor soils and a wet climate made it almost impossible, except on the islands of Tiree and Orkney, so it had to be imported. And, although peat was plentiful, the coal required to fire commercially viable stills also had to be brought in from elsewhere. As if all this were not difficult enough, the whisky then had to be delivered to its markets on the mainland.

However, despite the fierce winds and plentiful rain, the island winters are rarely severe and palm trees flourish in sheltered spots. The whiskies too have their own character, whether they are peated or unpeated, sweet or dry. Isle of Arran might still be taken for a Speyside, as it was in the 18th century, when the illicit malts of Glenlivet were compared to the equally glorious and equally illicit malts of Arran.

A NORTHERN OUTPOST

Lewis is the most northerly island in the Outer Hebrides and its landscape is wild and rugged, but Mark Tayburn was determined to find a way to supply everything for his whisky, 'from field to bottle'. An initial, successful planting of 10 acres of barley on distillery land is now supplemented by grain from Melbost Farms in Stornoway, on the far east of the island, where the coast is guarded by the Tiumpan Head lighthouse.

ABHAINN DEARG

Rich and smoky

Carnish, Isle of Lewis, HS2 9EX
www.abhainndearg.co.uk

Abhainn Dearg Distillery is famously remote. It sits in the hamlet of Uig, on the island of Lewis in the Outer Hebrides. The distillery's name – pronounced 'aveen jerrag' – means 'the red river' and it refers to a ferocious battle over 1,000 years ago between the local inhabitants of Lewis and a band of marauding Vikings. The locals succeeded in driving off the invaders, but there were so many casualties that the river ran red with blood.

Fortunately, the distillery has a much happier history. It was founded by a local man, Mark (Marco) Tayburn, in 2008, making it the first distillery to have been licensed in the Outer Hebrides since 1825, when Mackenzie of Seaforth began a small operation in Stornoway. Known as the Shoeburn Distillery, it operated for only 12 years. When the island was sold to Sir James Matheson, a teetotaller, in around 1840, most of it was knocked down to allow for the building of Lews Castle.

Illicit distilling continued on the island, however. Lewis had always had private distillers, even from the days before this was made illegal. Captain Edward Burt, an English officer serving in Scotland during the 1750s, recorded in his *Letters from a Gentleman in the North of Scotland* that 'The Collector of the Customs at Stornoway, in the Isle of Lewis, told me that about 120 families drink yearly 4,000 English gallons [18,180 litres] of *uisge beatha* [whisky] and brandy.'

The new distillery's production capacity, at around 10,000 litres per annum, is the smallest in Scotland and the whole operation is proudly artisanal. It is not Marco Tayburn's intention that 'the Lewis Malt' should ever become a global brand, rather 'the aim is to produce a quality single malt for those who take the trouble to visit us, support us via the Internet and, like the Shoeburn Distillery before us, supply local demand.'

▲ THE SPIRIT OF LEWIS
This, the first bottling from the distillery,
was released in September 2011 (at 3
years old) at the Royal National Gaelic
Mod – the festival of Gaelic music, arts
and culture – held that year at Stornoway.

◄ 'THE WITCHES' HATS'
Abhainn Dearg's stills, with crazily tilted
conical still heads and spidery lyne arms,
are unlike those of any other distillery in
Scotland. The design is based on that of
an illicit still found on the island in the
1950s and displayed at the distillery.

THE RED RIVER
Today the Abhainn Dearg rushes peacefully through stony moorland from Loch Raonasgail to the sea. It supplies the distillery with soft, mineral-rich water which is wonderfully pure: not a single dwelling sits between the water's source and the distillery.

UIG BEACH

The distillery is located in the hamlet of Uig, which sits around an inlet on the west coast of Lewis. Ancient hut circles were discovered on these beaches by archaeologists in the 1830s, along with the Lewis Chessmen – 93 chess pieces carved from walrus ivory and whales' teeth, dating back to the 11th century.

ISLE OF ARRAN

Flowers, pear drops and fresh apples

Lochranza, Isle of Arran, Isle Of Arran KA27 8HJ
www.arranwhisky.com

At one time the whiskies of Arran had a reputation equalled only by those of Glenlivet. This is somewhat mysterious, as the island only had one licensed distillery before the present one. That small affair sat in the small wooded glen at Lagg on the southeast coast; it was founded in 1825 and last heard of in 1837. So it seems that almost all of the legendarily fine whisky, known as 'the Arran waters', must have been illicit. Certainly, there are many stories about smuggling on the island, even in modern times. A fascinating book with the unprepossessing title of *The Statistical Account of Buteshire* (1841) describes the island as a 'stronghold of smuggling... which at one time afforded a sort of occupation for a great number of young men.'

The legal Isle of Arran Distillery now on the island was the brainchild of Harold Currie, former Managing Director of Chivas Brothers and later of Campbell Distillers, the Scotch whisky division of Pernod Ricard (which later acquired Chivas Brothers). It was commissioned in 1995 and is notable for being the only whisky distillery to open during that decade. To raise money for the venture, Mr Currie created

a 'founder's bonds' scheme, which guaranteed subscribers a quantity of whisky (five cases of blended Scotch in 1998 and five cases of Arran Founder's Reserve in 2001) instead of shares, in return for £450. The distillery sold all of the 2,500 available bonds within 18 months of making them available, but it is still possible today to buy casks of Arran new-make spirit.

There was much speculation in 1995 about what the style of Isle of Arran spirit would be, since the island lies between lowland Ayrshire and the Isle of Islay. Would it have a Lowland style, or a smoky Islay character, or maybe something in between, like, say, Talisker or Jura? As a Speyside distiller, Harold Currie wanted to create a fragrant, estery, Speyside style and this is still the hallmark of the Arran malt. However, since 2009 it has been joined by a peated expression, Machrie Moor, which was named after a famous site in the southwest of the island studded with standing stones and ancient remains. It is said that the warrior giant Fingal, king of the Caledonians, tethered his dog Bran to one of these stones, while boiling up his cauldron at the stone circle known as Fingal's Cauldron Seat.

▲ ARRAN OF THE MANY STAGS

The north part of the island is very mountainous and well populated by red deer, which sometimes come down to the beach at Lochranza. In folklore, the island was reputed to be a favourite hunting ground of the ancient Scottish king Fingal and his warriors. One 13th-century Irish poem begins:

Arran of the many stags,
The sea strikes against her shoulders,
Companies of men can feed there,
Blue spears are reddened among her
boulders.

◄ ALL IN ONE ROOM

The Isle of Arran Distillery is a perfect place to understand the distilling process, since all parts of it – mashing, fermenting and distilling – take place in a single spacious room. Another good reason for visiting is the visitor centre, opened by HM The Queen in 1997, which has won several awards. increasing capacity to 10 million litres.

▲ THE EASAN BIORACH

The water for Isle of Arran comes from Loch na Davie, high up in the mountains above the distillery, via the Easan Biorach. *Easan* is a waterfall in Gaelic and *biorach* is a heifer – and also a dog-fish. Take your pick!

◀ CAMPBELL LAING

Campbell Laing is the senior tour guide at the distillery – entertaining, hugely knowledgeable and full of local tales and lore. He stands here on a narrow path near the distillery that winds its way from the sea to the top of a dramatic bluff, with views over the northern coastline.

233

HIGHLAND PARK

Sweet malt, toffee and light smoke

Holm Road, Kirkwall KW15 1SU
www.highlandpark.co.uk

Said to have been founded in 1795 (although the bottle claims 1798), Highland Park lies on a hill overlooking Kirkwall on Orkney's main island. The original establishment was known as 'the High Park of Rosebank' and it was probably illicit. It was operated by a local brewer named Mansie (Magnus) Eunson, who was said by one source to be 'the greatest and most accomplished smuggler in Orkney'. Another source simply described him as 'a thug and small-time hood'. Whichever was true, Eunson enjoyed the protection of the provost (mayor) of Kirkwall, whose son took over the enterprise.

In 1813, Rosebank was divided into lots and sold. The portions containing the distillery were taken up by the local Collector of Excise, John Robertson, who had long pursued Mansie Eunson for tax. Although the district was now referred to as 'Highland Park', the distillery was named 'Kirkwall' until 1876. Another lot was taken by Robertson's son-in-law, Robert Borwick and in 1826 Borwick acquired the whole site and took out a license to distil. It was to remain in the Borwick family's ownership until 1869, when Robert's grandson, a minister of religion, sold it for £450 to a local farmer, because he believed that distilling was incompatible with his calling.

Production was greatly increased during the 1880s; Robertson & Baxter in Glasgow were appointed brokers and the make began to win a high reputation: a hogshead distilled in 1877 achieved a record price at auction in Edinburgh in 1892 and 12 years later no less an expert than Sir Alexander Walker (chairman of John Walker & Sons) wrote to R&B: 'I am in the process of conversion to the idea that Highland Park is the only whisky worth drinking and Johnnie Walker only fit for deluded Sassenachs!' In 1937, Highland Park was sold to R&B's sister company, Highland Distilleries. Both are now part of the Edrington Group and continue to promote this distinguished Orkney whisky vigorously.

235

◀ THE MALTINGS
Highland Park is one of only nine distilleries which malts a portion of its own barley on site, in traditional floor maltings, turning the malt by hand. The rest comes from independent maltsters on mainland Scotland and is blended with the distillery's own smoky malt.

◀ THE MALT KILN
In the 1970s the distillery experimented with buying in all their malt requirement from the mainland – malted to precisely their own peating levels. But the resulting spirit didn't taste the same, because the peat used to dry the 'green' malt was not Orcadian. They soon reverted to the 'old way'.

▲ THE VISITOR CENTRE
Although Highland Park malt has long had a high reputation, it was not promoted as a single until 1979. The first visitor centre was opened seven years later; it gradually expanded until 2000, when it was completely redesigned and awarded five stars by Visit Scotland. The year before, the United Nations had named the Orkney Islands a UNESCO World Heritage Site for its stone monuments dating back to 3000–2000 BCE.

JURA

Nut oil, pine sap, orange zest

Craighouse, Isle of Jura, Argyll PA60 7XT
www.jurawhisky.com

Jura is the wildest island in the Inner Hebrides, with very few people (about 190) and some stunning wildlife. Huge herds of red deer graze the valleys and flank the mountains, while birds of prey, such as golden eagles and sea eagles, patrol the skies. Otters and seals gambol about on the beaches and all in near-perfect silence, because there's only one, single-track road on the island.

It has never been easy to grow crops on the island's rocky terrain; some oats used to be grown and a dwarf barley called 'bere', but for centuries, most have been imported from Islay and Kintyre. Astonishingly, in spite of this, Jura had a licensed distillery by 1810 in Craighouse, the island's only village and the Jura distillery occupies the same site today.

The early distillery was a very small affair, but in 1831 it was enlarged by the local landowner, Archibald Campbell and managed by one Archibald Fletcher. Relations with the laird were rocky and times were hard – at one point Campbell thought of selling the stills for scrap to be able to pay the rent. Relations continued to be difficult with Fletcher's successors: one went bankrupt and the next removed all the distilling equipment and casks of whisky to Glasgow. This happened in 1901, when the population of Jura was over 1,000; by the 1950s it had dropped to 150. Two landowners on the island, Robin Fletcher and Tony Riley-Smith, realized they needed to rejuvenate it by providing more employment and they decided that one of the best ways to do this was to rebuild the distillery.

This made sound commercial sense. Demand for Scotch whisky had never been greater. Backing for the project came from Scottish & Newcastle Breweries and the old blending house, Charles Mackinlay & Company. In 1956 the landowners secured the services of William Delmé-Evans, who had built Tullibardine Distillery at Blackford, near Gleneagles, from scratch in the late 1940s. He designed stills to make spirit 'of a Highland character,' using malt that was only lightly peated, because this was more desired by the blenders than the smoky 'Islay-style.'

The first single malt from the new distillery was released in 1974 and the huge majority of the make went for blending. Of course, Islay-style malt is now very popular with whisky drinkers around the world and in response to this demand, Jura has, since 2002, offered a smoky style called 'Superstition.'

SMALL ISLES BAY

The village of Craighouse (seen in the distance) where the distillery is located, is situated on the south shore of Small Isles Bay, which gave its name to the original distillery on Jura. Although much of the island is wild and barren, there are many fine meadows, abundant with wildflowers. The gardens of Jura House, south of the village, are famous.

THE STILL HOUSE

The original still house built by Delmé-Evans contained only two stills, but a further pair were added under the management of Alan Rutherford in 1978. All the stills are of 'lantern shape' design, which drives heavier vapours back into the still, offering up only the light vapours that make up a soft 'Highland' style.

THE PERFECT SITE
Delmé-Evans used the same sloping site as the previous distillery, clearing the crumbling remains of the former, except for the manager's house (the tall building on the left). This has recently been refurbished and provides three handsome apartments for visitors. The water for distilling continues to come from the original source – the Market Loch or *Loch a'Bhaile Mhargaidh* – which lies in the hills behind Craighouse.

▲ LOMOND STILL

Lomond stills were invented in 1955 by Hiram Walker's production director to allow different styles of spirit to be made in a single still. They have an unusually broad neck, within which are set adjustable rectifying plates, similar to those found in patent stills. Rotating them to a horizontal position increases reflux and makes for a lighter spirit, while rotating to a vertical position results in the opposite.

SCENIC LOCATION ▶

The distillery takes its name from its location, close to Scapa Flow on Orkney Mainland. In 1887, whisky historian Alfred Barnard was moved to describe the 'beautiful seascape' around the distillery in more detail: 'sparkling in the bright sunshine are the white sails of ships and boats manned by crews who know every creek on the coast and whose voices can be heard singing the favourite *Orkney Boatman's Song*.'

SCAPA

Sweet malt, toffee and light smoke

St Ola, Kirkwall KW15 1SE
www.scapawhisky.com

Scapa Distillery overlooks Scapa Flow, one of Britain's most historic stretches of water. It connects the North Sea to the Atlantic Ocean, and forms a natural harbour that has been used since at least the 13th century (by Viking fleets) and proved a vital naval anchorage during the two World Wars. At the end of World War I, the captured German High Seas Fleet – 74 vessels – was interned there pending peace negotiations, and the ships were scuttled to prevent them falling into the hands of the British. In 1939, the tables were turned when a German U-boat managed to avoid the Flow's defences and sink battleship HMS *Royal Oak*.

Perhaps of most interest to whisky lovers, sailors of the Royal Navy saved the distillery from total destruction by fire in 1919 by forming a chain of buckets down to the sea. The owner at that time was the distillery's founder: a Glasgow whisky blender named John Townsend, who created Scapa in 1885. After the fire he sold the distillery and Scapa passed through several hands, including that of Hiram Walker Gooderham & Worts, the large Canadian distiller, who completely rebuilt it. All that remains of the Victorian distillery are two warehouses.

Hiram Walker also installed a Lomond-style wash-still (*see facing page*); its rectifying plates were removed in 1978 and replaced by a purifier. Similar stills were installed at Miltonduff and Inverleven Distilleries; Scapa's is the only one still remaining. Scapa may also have the longest fermentation time of any distillery, at 160 hours – most distilleries ferment for 48–65 hours. This makes a contribution to the flavour of the spirit, helping it develop fruity and floral flavours.

Ownership passed to Allied Distillers when they bought Hiram Walker in 1986, but Scapa's operations became sporadic: it was semi-mothballed for long periods and its occasional production was undertaken by staff from the nearby Highland Park Distillery. So it came as a surprise when, in 2004, the company embarked on a major refurbishment and began to promote Scapa as a single malt. Production was again halted in 2005 to allow for the completion of the refurbishment, but by the end of the year Pernod Ricard/Chivas Brothers were the new owners. All the whisky is now set aside to be used as single malt.

TALISKER

Maritime, with spice and smoke

Carbost, Isle of Skye IV47 8SR
www.discovering-distilleries.com

In 1880, the Scottish author Robert Louis Stevenson wrote a poem entitled 'The Scotsman's Return from Abroad', which included a reference to his much-missed malts:

> At last, across the weary faem,
> Frae far, outlandish pairts I came.
> On ilka side o' me I fand
> Fresh tokens o' my native land...
> But maistly thee, the bluid o' Scots,
> Frae Maidenkirk to John o' Grots,
> The king o' drinks, as I conceive it,
> Talisker, Isla, or Glenlivet!

Talisker was no doubt happy to have been among the writer's favourites, but it had had a difficult history since its foundation in 1830. The only distillery on the Isle of Skye, it was set up by the brothers Hugh and Kenneth MacAskill, who had arrived on Skye five years earlier from the small island of Eigg, some 80 miles south of Skye. They leased Talisker House and estate, a few miles outside the village of Carbost, from its owner, MacLeod of MacLeod. By 1830 they had raised £3,000, which was enough to build a distillery on the southern shore of Loch Harport with access to the sea. The distillery was not entirely welcomed in the local area; a former minister of the parish described its situation as 'one of the greatest curses that, in the ordinary course of Providence, could befall [Carbost] or any other place'.

Kenneth MacAskill died in 1854, by which time Talisker had acquired quite a reputation. The distillery was put up for sale for £1,000, a knockdown price that reflected the gloomy state of the whisky trade. However, no buyer was found, and Hugh ran the distillery until he died in 1863 when the lease was transferred to his son-in-law, Donald MacLennan. Unfortunately, MacLennan went bankrupt the same year. The distillery was then taken on by one J R W Anderson, who seems to have fallen victim to the same bad luck or judgement; he was imprisoned in 1880 for defrauding customers, taking money from them for non-existent whisky that he had promised to hold in bonded warehouses for them.

The new owners were men of substance: Alexander Grigor Allan, solicitor and part-owner of Glenlossie Distillery, and Roderick Kemp, wine and spirits merchant in Aberdeen. They rebuilt Talisker and modernized it, but in 1892 the partnership was dissolved. Allan bought out Kemp, who acquired Macallan Distillery, and incorporated The Talisker Distillery Co Ltd, which merged with The Dailuaine

TALISKER HOUSE
The MacAskill brothers leased Talisker House from the MacLeods, whose former guests included the authors Samuel Johnson and James Boswell, as documented in Boswell's *The Journal of a Tour to the Hebrides with Samuel Johnson* (1785).

PURE WATER SOURCE
Talisker's process water comes from a burn which rises in the Cnoc nan Speireag ('Hawkhill'). Its cooling water is taken from the Carbost Burn, which rises on the peaty saddle separating the village from Gleann Oraid. The water from Carbost Burn was also used to drive a waterwheel, supplementing power from a steam engine.

Distillery Co Ltd in 1898, with Thomas Mackenzie (of Dailuaine) as managing director.

On Mackenzie's death in 1916, the majority of the shares in Dailuaine-Talisker were acquired by the 'Big Three' – Dewar's, Walker's and Buchanan's – with the DCL, and when these companies all amalgamated in 1925, Talisker joined the DCL.

The still house was destroyed by fire in 1960, and this led to a major rebuilding programme over the following two years, although Talisker's five oddly shaped stills were copied exactly so as not to change the uniquely spicy flavour of the spirit. Today the majority of the whisky goes into blends – it is a key component in Johnnie Walker Red Label, the world's bestselling Scotch – but a small amount has always been released as a single malt, and the make's fame and popularity spread when it was chosen by United Distillers (now Diageo) to represent the 'island' style in their Classic Malts selection.

▲ **SPIRIT OF THE SEA**
Most of Talisker's spirit is
tankered to Central Scotland
for maturation, but around
4,500 casks still remain on
site. Wherever the spirit is
matured, it still has briny,
maritime characteristics,
perpetuating the debate
about the source of whisky's
saltiness. Where does it
come from, if not from the
microclimate of the seaside
warehouse?

UNIQUE LYNE ARMS ▶
The lyne arms connecting
the stills to the worm tubs
at Talisker curve round in
an inverted U-bend. They
are also fitted with purifier
pipes, which increases reflux
substantially and is unique in
the industry.

247

TOBERMORY

Malty, maritime, nutty

Ledaig, Tobermory PA75 6NR
www.tobermorydistillery.com

Tobermory village, on the Isle of Mull, came into being quite deliberately: it was planned by the British Fisheries Society (BFS) in 1788. This august body of (mainly) Scottish aristocrats who lived in London wanted to create new fishing communities in remote parts of North Britain and they had the full support of the British government. The BFS had been founded two years previously, with the Duke of Argyll as its first Governor and the Marquess of Breadalbane as its Deputy Governor. The foundation of Tobermory and Ullapool were its earliest projects; later it would create 'the largest herring port in the world' at Pulteneytown, Wick (*see* Old Pulteney, *pp. 112–13*).

The main attraction of Tobermory was its natural harbour, affording shelter in all weathers. This part of the site was owned by the Duke of Argyll, who offered it to the Society at a knockdown rent. The designer was Robert Mylne, with adjustments proposed by Thomas Telford, the Society's Chief Engineer. The main contractors were Hugh and John Stevenson, the founders of Oban and its distillery (*see* Oban, *pp. 144–5*).

Unfortunately, Tobermory turned out to be too far from the fishing grounds to be much use as a fishing port, but it quickly became the principal trading port on Mull. It was greatly assisted by the enormous increase in the kelp trade from the Hebrides and by the opening of the Crinan Canal in 1801.

The ash from burnt kelp, called soda ash, was a key ingredient in glass-making and among those who made their fortunes from kelp was one John Sinclair. He had arrived at Tobermory in the early 1790s and set up as a merchant. In 1797, Sinclair applied to the directors of the BFS to lease 57 acres to the south of the harbour front, in a district named Ledaig, on which he wished to build houses, a pier and a distillery. The original distillery was named Ledaig and today a heavily peated expression of the malt from the Tobermory Distillery uses this name.

The subsequent history of Ledaig Distillery is patchy, with several tenants and periods of closure. It did not really stabilize until the current owners, Burn Stewart Distillers, bought it in 1993. They have opened an attractive small visitor centre and have rationalized the branding, which had become confused – an earlier owner had bottled 'Tobermory' as both a blended whisky and a blended malt and 'Ledaig' (in very small amounts) as a single malt. Today, both are fine single malts.

THE MISHNISH LOCHS
The village of Tobermory derives its name from *Tobar Mhairi*, 'St Mary's Well', an ancient holy well in the village. However, the distillery takes its process water from lochs in the hills behind the town, via the Mishnish Burn. The water is heavily peated, often of a dark red hue and this may contribute to the whisky's slight smokiness.

1 A MODEL VILLAGE

Tobermory is a model village – and this has nothing to do with it being chosen to represent Balamory in the successful children's TV series! Nor does it have anything to do with its picture postcard situation and gaily painted houses. It was planned and built as a fishing port, although it turned out to be too far from the fishing grounds to attract many fishermen.

2 THE ORIGINAL HAMLET

Until the new village was built, the only settlement here was a farming hamlet high above the bay, around the early medieval church and well of St Mary (*Tobar Mhairi*). In the 1870s, the Reverend John Marius Wilson described it in *The Imperial Gazetteer of England and Wales* as having 'much celebrity in the days of popery'. The surrounding country is wild and windswept.

3 A TRADITIONAL DISTILLERY

There is much that is traditional at the Tobermory Distillery. It has an old-fashioned, cast-iron rake-and-plough mash tun with a copper canopy, four Douglas fir washbacks and two pairs of 'boil-ball' stills crammed into its tiny still house.

4 ESTABLISHED 1798

The outside wall of the small visitor centre proudly emphasizes that the distillery dates from the late 18th century. Its founder, John Sinclair, did not receive the charter to the land until 1823 and this is given as the foundation date by whisky historian Alfred Barnard.

INDEX

Entries in *italics* refer to illustrations.

Aberdeen 76, 119, 130, 166, 188, 244
Aberdeen Angus cattle *31*
Aberdeenshire 13, 119, 127
Aberfeldy Distillery 56–9, *57*
Aberlour Distillery 154, *154–7*, 193, 196
Abernethy steam engines 161
Abhainn Dearg Distillery *224–9*, 225
Ainslie & Co 98
Albany, Robert Stewart, Duke of 69
Albert, Prince Consort 135
alcohol content 8–9
Alexander III, King of Scotland 100
Allan, Alexander Grigor 244
Allardice, James 123–4
Allied Distillers 95, 124, 243
Alness 100
Anderson, J R W 244
The Angels' Share (movie) 48, 70
Angus 13, 119
aqua vitae 29
Ardbeg Distillery *28–31*, 29–30, 37
Ardross Estate 100
Argyll, Duke of 248
Argyll, Marquess of *142*
Arkwright, Richard *68*, 69
Arran, Isle of 223, 230, *231–3*
Asahi Breweries Ltd 140
Associated Scottish Distillers 120
Atholl, Dukes of 61, *62*, 72
Atholl, Forest of 66
Auchentoshan Distillery *14–17*, 15
Aultmore Distillery 158–9, *159–61*, 170

Bacardi Corporation 57, 159
Badenoch 55
Balblair Distillery *94*, 95, 103, 112
Ballechin Distillery 75
Ballindalloch Castle 178, *179*, 180, 183
Balmoral Castle 135, *137*
Balvenie Castle 186

Balvenie Distillery 162, 163–5, *191*
Ban, Loch nam 43
Banff 95
Barclay, Jimmy 217
barley 8, *44*
malting 8, *46*, *53*, 148, 237
Barnard, Alfred 27, *41*, 43, 48, 76, 95, 103, 112, 120, *122*, 145, 147, *148*, *155*, 174, *181*, *182*, *194*, 212, *221*, *242*, *251*
barrels 11, *17*, *20*, 35, *59*, 103, 123, 140, *148*, 151, *206*
Beaton family 29
Begg, John 135–6
Bell, Arthur & Sons 61–2
Ben Nevis Distillery 140, *141–3*
Ben Vrackie 61
BenRiach Distillery 124, 166, *167–9*
Benrinnes Distillery 170, *182*
Benromach Distillery 170–1, *171–3*
Berry Bros & Rudd 39, *207*
Beveridge, Jim 176
Black Isle 93
Blackford 69, 88, *91*
Blair Athol Distillery *60–3*, 61
Blair Castle 61, *62*
Blairgar Burn 77
boats, 'puffers' *28*, *38*
boil-ball spirit stills *47*, *113*, *133*, *164*, *251*
Bon Accord Distillery 166
Borwick, Robert 235
Boswell, James *245*
bottling 45, 57, *59*, 74, 149, 151, *162*, *194*
Bouch, Sir Thomas 204
Bowmore Distillery 27, 32, *33*, 36, 126, 217
Braeval 64
Breadalbane, Marquis of 57, *248*
Brickmann, F W (Walter) 170
British Empire Exhibition (1924) *18*

British Fisheries Society (BFS) 112, 248
Brodie Hepburn 69–70, 88
Broom, Dave 6
Brora 96, *97*, 98, *98*
Brown, James 37
Bruichladdich Distillery *34–7*, 35–6, *151*
Buchan 119
Buchanan, Thomas Grey 30
Buchanan-Dewar 176
Bulloch, John 15
Bulloch Lade & Company 39, 43, 224
Bunnahabhain Distillery 37, *38–41*, 39, 45, 204
Burghead 174
Burn Stewart Distillers 70, 248
Burns, Robert 19, 120
Burt, Captain Edward 225
Bushmills Distillery 149
butts 11, *17*, *63*, 103, *151*, 156, *206*
Byron, Lord 135

Cadboll Stone *107*
Cadenhead's 149
Cairngorms *66*
Caledonian Alps *137*
Caledonian Bank 184, 204, 220
Cameron, Alexander 57
Campari 194
Campbell, Archibald 238
Campbell, Clan 29
Campbell, Daniel 32
Campbell, S & Son 154
Campbell, Walter Frederick 29, 32
Campbell Distillers 74, 230
Campbeltown 8, 39, 139, 147, *148*, 149
Caol Ila Distillery 39, *42*, 43, 98
Carbost Burn *246*
Cardhu Distillery 174, *175–7*, 209
Carn Liath *198*
casks 11, *151*, *168*, *191*, *206*, *221*
Castle Leod 100
cats *82*
cattle *31*, 45, 51, 85, 115

Celtic High Crosses *30*
Chivas Brothers 118, 124, *168*, 217, 230, 243
Clyde, River 15, 43, 76
Clydebank 15
Clynelish Distillery 96–7, *97–9*
Cockburn, John 19
Columba, St 154
Comyn, John 'The Black' *142*
Connacher, Alexander 61
Conval Hills *164*, 186, *191*
Cook & Bernheimer 64
Costello, Frank 72
Cowan, Alexander 95
Cragganmore Distillery 178–80, *179–81*
Craig, Charles 95
Craigellachie Distillery 158, 170
Craighouse 238, *239*
Crieff 64
Cromartie, Earl of 100
Cromarty Firth 100, *101*
Cruickshank, John 204
Culloden, Battle of (1746) 61
Cumming, Elizabeth 174, 176, 186
Cumming, John and Helen 174
Cumming, John Fleetwood 176
Cumming, Lewis 174
Cumming, Robert 'Bertie' 95, 112
Cumming, Ronald 176
Cupar 23
Currie, Harold 230
Customs and Excise, HM *74*
Cuthbert, Ian and Francis 23

Daftmill Distillery *22–5*, 23
Dailey, J J & Sons 72
Dailuaine Distillery *56*, *244–6*
Dalgarno, Bob 215
Dalmore Distillery 100, *101*, 103
Dalvey Distillery 153
Dalwhinnie Distillery 64, *65–7*

Deanston Distillery 68–71, 69–70
Dee, River 135
Delmé-Evans, William 88, 89, 238, 240, 241
Depression (1930s) 62, 130, 220
Dewar, John & Sons 56, 57, 58, 109, 159, 220
Dewar, John Alexander 57
Dewar, Sir Thomas (Tommy) 57, 59, 184
Diageo 11, 19, 43, 48, 62, 98, 109, 136, 145, 159, 176, 209, 210, 246
Dick, Robert 204
Distillers Company Ltd (DCL) 19, 43, 48, 58, 62, 64, 85, 98, 109, 126, 130, 136, 145, 159, 168, 170, 176, 180, 198, 209, 246
Doig, Charles Cree 58, 64, 78, 158, 163, 166, 170, 178, 183, 191, 204–6, 209
Dornoch Firth 95, 103, 106
Doune 69
Doune Castle 70, 71
draff 28, 41, 45, 83
Dronac Burn 122
Drostan, St 154
Drummond, John 81
Duff, John 166
Dufftown 178, 186, 191
Dufftown Distillery 63
Dumbarton 76
Dumgoyne Hill 76
Dundas Hill 35
dunnage warehouses 11, 23, 202, 221
Dunnet Bay 116
Durham & Company 103
Durie, David 120
Durie, James 120

Earn, River 55
Easan Biorach 233
East Lothian 19
Easter Elchies House 213
Easter Ross 103
Edderton 95
Edinburgh 19, 62, 66, 100, 123, 196, 204, 220, 235
Edradour Distillery 43, 76, 81, 82, 212, 235
Edrington Group 43, 76, 81, 82, 212, 235
Edward, Prince of Wales 136, 140
Edward, Alexander 145, 158, 170, 180
The 1887 Company Ltd 81
Elgin 130, 201, 202
Elizabeth II, Queen of England 136, 210, 232

Emperador Group 120
Eunson, Mansie (Magnus) 235
Excise Act (1823) 123, 135, 153

Fairlie, James 81
Falkirk 64, 139
Falkland Palace 25
The Famous Grouse 39, 43, 81, 82, 204
Fasque Estate 120
feints 10, 47, 168
Fenella 120
Ferintosh Distillery 93
fermentation 8–9, 16, 58, 75, 110, 176, 184, 232, 243
Fettercairn Distillery 119, 120, 121
Fiddich, River 186, 187
Fife 23
Fife, Dukes of 130, 158, 186
Fife, William Duff, 1st Earl of 162
Filshie, Alexander 15
Findhorn, River 85, 170
Fingal 230, 232
Fionnaidh Burn 108
Fleming, James 154
Fletcher, Archibald 238
Fletcher, Robin 238
Flow Country 115
Foggie Moss 158, 159
Forbes, Duncan (Edradour) 72
Forbes, Duncan (Ferintosh) 93
foreshots 10, 47, 168
Forfarshire 119
Forres 145, 170
Fort William 145

Gandhi, Dhavali 215
The Garioch 118, 126
George III, King of England 210
George IV, King of England 196
germinating grains 8–9, 46, 53
Gesner, Konrad 115
Gibbs, James 162
Gilbey, W & A Ltd 209
gin 36, 104
Giovinetti, Armando 194
Gladstone, Sir John 120
Glasgow 14, 15, 32, 35, 36, 39, 43, 48, 51, 58, 69, 76, 88, 98, 100, 120, 126, 138, 145, 204, 235, 238, 243
Glen Garioch Distillery 126, 127–9

Glen Grant Distillery 154, 192–5, 193–4
Glen Moray Distillery 200–3, 201
Glen Ord Distillery 43, 93, 108–11, 109, 110
Glen Scotia Distillery 147
Glenallachie Distillery 88
Glendronach Distillery 122–5, 123–4, 166
Glenfarclas Distillery 178, 182–5, 183–4, 188
Glenfiddich Distillery 81, 124, 151, 162, 164, 186–8, 187–91, 193
Glengoyne Distillery 76, 77–9, 220
Glengyle Distillery 149
Glenkinchie Distillery 18–21, 19
Glenlivet 8, 61, 124, 153, 154, 166, 178, 180, 183–4, 194, 196–8, 197–9, 201, 204, 212, 223, 230, 244
Glenlossie Distillery 166, 244
Glenmorangie Distillery 30, 102–7, 103–4, 201
Glenrothes Distillery 39, 81, 204–6, 205–7, 220
Glenturret Distillery 80–3, 81
Gloag, Matthew 81, 82
Gordon, Dukes of 123, 196
Gordon, James 154
Gordon & Macphail (G&M) 170–1, 172
grain whisky 13, 55, 91, 196
Grampian Mountains 120, 166
Grant, Captain Charles 124
Grant, George 183–4
Grant, J & G Ltd 184
Grant, James 154, 193
Grant, James Jnr 193
Grant, John (Glenfarclas) 183–4
Grant, John (Aberlour and Glen Grant) 154, 193
Grant, Captain John 213
Grant, William (Balvenie) 162
Grant, William (Glenfiddich) 186, 188, 188, 191
Grant, William (Tamdhu) 220
Grant, William & Co 204
Grant, William & Sons 81, 163, 186
Great Depression (1930s) 62, 130, 220
Great North of Scotland Railway 87, 130, 158
green malt 9, 46, 52, 53, 110, 191, 237

Greenlees Brothers 39
grist mills 9, 133
Guinness plc 62

Haig, John & Company 19
Haim, Irving 72
Harvey, John 35
Harvey, Robert 35
Harvey, Rudd 35
Harvey, William 35
Harvey McNair & Co 170
Hay, Robert 183
Hazelburn Distillery 39, 149
heads 10
'heart of the run' 10, 168
Hebrides 224, 225, 238, 245, 248
Helen, Fair Queen 88
Hempriggs, Loch of 112
Henderson, Hector 43
Henderson, James & Company 112
Hermelin, Otto 37
Highland cattle 30
Highland Distilleries 39, 76, 204, 207, 212, 220, 235
Highland Line 13, 76, 118
Highland Park Distillery 43, 81, 212, 234–7, 235, 243
Highland Railway Company 87
'Highland style' malts 8
Highlands 6, 13
  Central Highlands 54, 55–91
  East Highlands 118, 119–37
  North Highlands 92, 93–117
  West Highlands 138, 139–51
Hill Thomson and Co 194
Hiram Walker 30, 95, 243
Hobbs, Joseph 140, 142
Hogg, James 196
hogsheads 11, 17, 20, 63, 151, 206
Howe o'Fife 25
Hunter, Ian 51–2, 52

Imperial Distillery 220
Indaal, Loch 34
International Distillers & Vintners (IDV) 209
Inver House Distillers 95, 112, 131
Invergordon Distillers 70, 88, 149
Inverleven Distillery 36, 243
Inverlochy Castle 142
Inverness 87, 94
Iona 145
Isla, River 158
Islands 222, 223–51

Islay 8, *26*, 27–53
Islay, Sound of 39, *40*,
    42, 43
Islay Distillers 39
'Islay style' malts 8
Isle of Arran Distillery 223,
    230, *231–3*

Jacobites 61, 93
James IV, King of Scotland
    29, 88, *91*
James VI, King of Scotland
    115
Jardine, William 100
Jardine Matheson & Co
    100
'Joe' 75
Johnson, Samuel 245
Johnston, Donald and
    Alexander 51
Johnston, Dugald 51
Johnston, John 48
juniper 85
Jura 39, 43, 88, 223, 230,
    238, *239–41*
Justerini & Brooks (J & B)
    209, *210*

Kemp, Roderick 212, 244
Kenneth III, King of Scots
    120
Kilchoman Distillery 27, 29,
    33, *37*, 44–7, 45, *151*
Kildalton Cross 30
Killiecrankie, Battle of
    (1689) 61
kilns 9, 32, 45, *46*, 52, 53,
    73, *110*, *163*, 187, *191*,
    209, 237
Kintyre peninsula 139
Kirkwall 235
Knock 130
Knock Hill 130
Knockando Distillery 131,
    208–11, 209, 220
Knockdhu Distillery 130–1,
    131–3
Kokubu & Company 85

La Martiniquaise 201
La Reserve, Soho, London
    35
Lagavulin Distillery 29, 48,
    49, 51, 180
Laing, Campbell *233*
Laing, Robin 6
Lairg 139
Lang, Alexander and
    Gavin 76
Laphroaig Distillery 27, 29,
    48, *50–3*, 51–2
Latheron 112
Lauter mash tuns *91*, *129*
Ledaig Distillery 248
Leishman, Thomas *121*

Leith 72, 103, *127*, 159,
    170, 174, 176, 183,
    201, 209
Leslie, Lady Mary *205*
Lewis 223, *224*, 225,
    227, *229*
Linkwood Distillery 154
Littlemill Distillery 43
Loach, Ken 48, 70
Loch, James 96
Lochnagar, Royal *134–7*,
    135–6
Lochranza Bay *232*
Lomond, Loch 55
Lomond Hills 25
Lomond stills *242*
Longmore, William 217
Longmorn Distillery 166,
    167
Longrow Distillery 149
Lossie, River 166
Lour Burn 154
low wines 10, *79*
Lowlands 7, *12*, 13–25
lyne arms *113*, *161*, 227,
    247

Macallan Distillery 43,
    81, 178, 212, *213–15*,
    220, 244
Macallum, Duncan 170
MacAskill, Hugh and
    Kenneth 244, *245*
MacBeatha family 29
Macbeth *202*
Macdonald, Aeneas 153
MacDonald, Angus Og 29
Macdonald, Donald Peter
    140
Macdonald, 'Long John'
    140
Macdonald & Muir (M & M)
    103, 104, 201
Macdonald Greenlees 64
MacDougall, Alexander 30
MacDougall, John 29–30
McDowell, R J S 112
McEwan, James 36, 37
McHardy, Frank 149
Mackenzie, Alexander 109
Mackenzie, Andrew 100
Mackenzie, Charles 100
Mackenzie, Peter & Co. 62
Mackenzie, Thomas 109,
    246
Mackenzie, William 100
Mackenzie of Seaforth 225
McKerrow, Neil 103
Mackessack, Douglas 194
Mackie, J L & Co. 48, 51
Mackie, James Logan 48
Mackie, Sir Peter 48, 51,
    170, 180
Mackinlay, Charles &
    Company 176, 238

MacLachlan, John &
    George 15
Maclellan, John 45
McLennan, Alexander 109
MacLennan, Donald 244
Macleod, Ian & Company
    76, 242
Macpherson-Grant, Sir
    George 178
Maison Michel Picard 89
Malcolm, Dennis 194
Malt Mill 48
malting barley 8, *46*, 53,
    148, 237
Manson, John 126
Manson, Sir Patrick 126
Margadale Hills 39
Marubeni Corporation 85
mash tuns 9, *16*, 35, 36,
    41, 71, *83*, *91*, 109, *124*,
    129, 140, *144*, *172*, 199,
    201, *251*
mashing 8–9, *41*, *83*, 157
Matheson, Alexander 100,
    103
Matheson, Sir James 100,
    225
Matheson, William *102*, 103
maturing whisky 8, 11, *17*,
    20, 33, 36, *37*, *42*, *63*,
    103, *110*, *113*, 119, 140,
    151, 156, 202, 215, 218,
    221, 247
Mearns country 119, 120
milling 9
Milne, Alexander 217
Milne, Jane 158
Milton 19
Miltonduff Distillery 209, 243
Mishnish Loch *249*
Mitchell, Ian 156
Mitchell, J & A 147, 149
Mitchell, John and William
    147
Moët Hennessy 103
Monadhliath Mountains
    66, 85
Montrose, Marquess of *142*
Moray, James Stewart,
    'Bonnie Earl of' 71
Moray Firth 162, 174
Morrison, John 130
Morrison, Stanley P 15,
    32, 126
Morrison Bowmore Distillers
    15, 36, 126
Mortlach Distillery 186
Mull, Isle of 223, 248
Munro, James & Sons 64
Murray, Dr Douglas 11
Murray family 88
Murray McDavid 35, 36
Mutch, Neil 126
Mutter, James and William
    32
Mylne, Robert 248

The National Distillers of
    America 120
Ness, River 140
New Keith 217
New Pitsligo Moss 126,
    162
Nikka Whisky Distilling
    Company 140

oak casks 11, *17*, *191*,
    206, *221*
Oban Distillery 139, *144*,
    145, 170, 248
Ochil Hills 55, 88
Octomore Farm, Port
    Charlotte 37
Okura 85
Old Kilpatrick Hills 15
Old Pulteney Distillery 95,
    112, *113*
Oldmeldrum 126
onion stills *42*, *63*, *161*, 200
Orkney 223, 235, *237*, 243
Ormiston estate 19

pagoda ventilators *22*, *52*,
    73, *78*, *110*, *163*, 170,
    191, 209
Paps of Jura *40*, *42*
Parkmore Distillery 178
Pattison's of Leith 183–4,
    209
peat 6, 9, 27, 32, *46*, 48,
    53, 55, 74, 85, 115, 126,
    130, 149, *159*, 162, 184,
    224, 237
Pedro Ximénez sherry 17
Pencaitland 19
Pennan 162
Pentland Firth *116*
Pernod Ricard 124, 154,
    194, 217, 230, 243
Perth 55, 57, 81
Perthshire 13
pH values, water 8
Pictish monuments 107
Pitilie Burn 57, *58*
Pitlochry 61, 62, *74*
Pollo Distillery 95
Pomeroy, Jay 217
Port Askaig 39, *41*, 43
Port Ellen Maltings 27, 45
port pipes *151*
Porteus Company *202*
pot stills 13, *18*, *164*
process water 8, *37*, 39,
    69, 88, *98*, 108, 109,
    122, 154, *164*, *246*, *249*
Prohibition 72, 140, 198
'puffers' (boats) *28*, *38*
'puggies' (steam trains)
    56, *167*
Pulteney, Sir William 112
Pulteney Distillery 95,
    112, *113*

Pultneytown 112, 248
puncheons 11, *151*

railways *56*, *87*, *94*, 95,
   130, 158, 160, 170,
   179, 192
'rake-and-plough' mash
   tuns *71*, *124*, *144*, *251*
Ramsay, Sir Alexander 120
Rate, John and George 19
refill hogsheads 11, *20*, *163*
Reid, Alexander 212
Reid, William 147
Rémy Cointreau *37*, 81
Reynier, Mark 35, 36
Riechlachan Distillery 147
Riley-Smith, Tony 238
Risk, John 98
Robbie Dhu Springs *164*,
   186, *191*
Robertson, George 61
Robertson, James of
   Crathie 135
Robertson, John 235
Robertson, Robert 61
Robertson, W A 204
Robertson, William 39
Robertson & Baxter (R & B)
   39, 43, 76, 204, 220,
   235
Ross, Andrew 95
Ross, John 95
Ross, W H 209
Rothes 154, 193, *205*
Royal Lochnagar Distillery
   134–7, 135–6
Royal Navy 243
Rutherford, Alan *240*

Saintsbury, George 96
Saladin boxes 220
Sanderson, William & Co
   220
Sanquhar Estate 145, 170
Scapa Distillery *242*, 243
Scapa Flow *242*, 243
Schenley Corporation 52
'Scotch malt whisky' 8
Scott, Andy *71*
Scott, Sir Walter 61, *71*
Scott, Walter 124
Scottish & Newcastle
   Breweries 238
Scottish Malt Distillers
   (SMD) 19, *58*, 97, 98,
   145
Seafield, Earls of 212,
   213, 217
Seagram *168*, 194, *216*,
   217
Sharp's Brewery 88
sherry casks 11, *17*, 119,
   151, *156*, 191, *206*,
   215, 221
Shoeburn Distillery 225

Signatory Vintage Scotch
   Whisky 74
Simson, David 32
Simson, Hector 32
Sinclair, John 248
Skye, Isle of 76, 145, 212,
   220, 223, 244
Smith, George 154, 178,
   196
Smith, George & J G Ltd
   194
Smith, Gordon 178
Smith, John 178, *179*, 183
Smith, John Gordon 196
Smith, Mary Jane 180
Smith Grant, Captain Bill
   198
Smokehead 76
smoky whisky 8, 9, 27,
   39, 43, 46, 51, 93, 119,
   230, 238
Society of Improvers of
   Knowledge of Agriculture
   19
Spey, River *175*, *181*, 209,
   220
Speyside 8, 147, *152*,
   153–221
Speyside Cooperage *206*
Speyside Railway 178,
   179, 193
Spiller, Brian 176
spirit receivers 10
spirit stills *24*, *47*, *67*, *79*,
   91, 100, *101*, *113*, *114*,
   131, *151*, 162, *168*,
   188, *215*
Springbank Distillery
   146–51, 147–9
Staffa 145
Staoinsha, Loch 39
steam engines 69, 138,
   161, *246*
Stevenson, Hugh 145, 248
Stevenson, John 145, 248
Stevenson, Robert 145
Stevenson, Robert Louis
   244
Stewart, John 61
stills 10
   boil-ball spirit stills *47*,
      113, *133*, *164*, *251*
   Lomond stills *242*
   onion stills *42*, *63*, *161*,
      200
   pot stills 13, *18*, *164*
   sight-glasses *84*
   spirit stills *24*, *47*, *67*, *79*,
      91, 100, *101*, *113*, *114*,
      131, *151*, 162, *168*,
      188, *215*
   wash stills 10, *24*, *33*,
      47, *67*, 74, *79*, 84,
      100, *101*, *113*, *151*,
      161, 162, 194, *215*,
      219, 243

Stornoway *224*, 225, *227*
Strathearn 55
Strathisla Distillery 153,
   216–19, 217
Strathspey Distillery 64
Strathspey Railway 171
Stuart, James 212
Suntory 15, 32, 52, 126,
   212
Sutherland, Dukes of 96,
   100
Symington, Andrew 74, 75

tails 10
Tain 95, 103
Takara Shuzo 85
Talisker Distillery 212,
   244–6, *245–7*
Tamdhu Distillery 76, 209,
   220, *221*
Tay, River 55, 158, 204
Tayburn, Mark (Marco)
   224, 225
Taylor, George 217
Teacher, William & Sons
   124
Teaninich Distillery 124
Teith, River *68*, 69
Telford, Thomas 112, 154,
   248
terroir 6, 36
Thompson, John Tytler 209
Thomson, J G & Co *127*
Thorne, R & Sons 154
Thurso *94*, 115
Tiree 223
Tobermory Distillery 248,
   249–51
Tomatin Distillery *84–7*, 85
Torran, Loch an *37*
Townsend, John 243
triple distillation *17*, 149
Trossachs 55, 69
Truim, River *65*
Tullibardine Distillery 69,
   88–9, *89–91*, 238
Tummel, River 55
Turney, J G & Son 72
Turret, River 81

Uig 225, *229*
uisge beatha 29, 225
Ullapool 248
United Breweries Group *121*
United Distillers 180, 246
Urquhart, George 170–1
Urquhart, John 170–1
Usher, Andrew 196

Victoria, Queen *31*, 61, 135,
   137, 140
Vikings 225, 243

Wade, General George
   64, *65*

Walker, Sir Alexander 176,
   235
Walker, Billy 124, 166
Walker, John & Sons 98,
   176, *177*, 220
warehouses 11, 15, *20*, *23*,
   33, 36, *37*, *42*, 43, *50*,
   63, *70*, 74, 75, 76, *91*,
   97, 98, 145, *156*, *168*,
   181, 184, 201, *202*, *210*,
   218, *221*, 243, 244, *247*
wash 9, 75
wash stills 10, *24*, *33*, *47*,
   67, 74, *79*, 84, 100, *101*,
   113, *151*, *161*, 162, 194,
   215, *219*, 243
washbacks 9, *16*, 36, 48,
   71, *91*, 109, *110*, *124*,
   129, *172*, *184*, 201, 251
water 8
water towers *25*
waterwheels 43, *68*, 69,
   112, 136, *161*, 194,
   219, *246*
Watson, James & Co 109,
   178
Watt, James 69
Welles, Orson 34
Western Isles 27, 145
'Whisky Boom' 39, 72, 85,
   153, 158, 162, 193, 220
Whitbread plc 140
White Horse Distillers 180
Whitely, William & Co 72
Whittaker, James 52
Whyte & Mackay 88–9,
   100, 120
Wick 95, 112, 248
Wilks, Cathy 45
Williams, William &
   Company 188
Williamson, Bessie 52
Wills, Anthony 45
Wilson, Rev John Marius
   251
Wine & Spirit Association
   215
Wishaw Distillery 178
Wolf of Badenoch *205*
Wolfburn Distillery *114–17*,
   15
World War I 147, 170, 180,
   198, 243
World War II 15, 88, *142*,
   199
worm tubs *20*, 64, *67*, 74,
   113, *131*, *133*, *144*, *151*,
   180, *247*
wort 9

yeast 8
Yoker distillery 35

CREDITS

Every effort has been made to contact copyright holders. However, the publishers will be glad to rectify in future editions any inadvertent omissions brought to their attention.
Key: a – above; b – below; c – centre; l – left; r – right

COMMISSIONED PHOTOGRAPHY FOR FRANCES LINCOLN

© Allan MacDonald: 1, 2–3, 7, 10, 14, 16 a&b, 17 a&b, 38, 40, 41 a&c&b, 42 a&b, 50, 52, 53 l&r, 56, 58 a&b, 59 a&b, 65, 66 a&b, 67, 68, 70, 71 a&b, 80, 82 l&r, 83, 84, 86 a&b, 8 7a&b, 89, 90, 91, 94, 97, 98, 99, 101 a&c, 102, 104, 105, 106, 107, 108, 110, 111, 113 a&b, 114, 116, 117, 121, 122, 124, 125 a&b, 127, 128 a&b, 129, 131, 132 a&b, 133, 141, 142, 143, 146, 148 a&b, 151, 159, 160 a&b, 161 l&r, 167, 168 l&r, 169, 175, 176, 177 a&b, 187, 188, 189, 190 a&bl&br, 191, 200, 202, 203 a&b, 208, 210 a&b, 211, 214, 215 l&r, 221 a&b, 224, 226 al&ar&b, 227, 228, 229, 234, 236 a&b, 237, 242 a&b, 245, 246 a&b, 247, 249, 250 al&ar, 251
© Lara Platman: 18, 20 b, 21, 22, 24, 28, 30, 31, 33 a&c&b, 44, 46 a&b, 47 a&b, 49 a&b, 73, 74, 75a, 77, 78, 79 a&b, 134, 136 l&r, 144 b, 150 a&b, 156 b, 157, 163, 171, 179, 180, 181, 182, 185 a&b, 192, 195 b, 205, 206, 216, 218 a, 231, 232 b, 233 a&b, 239, 240

ADDITIONAL MATERIAL

age footstock 195 a; Alamy: adp-stock 20 a; Benromach Distillery 172 a&b, 173 a&c&b; Bruichladdich Distillery 37 a&bl&br; Dalmore Distillery 101 b; David Burton 250 b; David Chapman 197; David Gowans 164; Dennis Hardley 62; Doug Houghton 25 a; Francis Cuthbert 25 b; Glenrothes Distillery 207 a&b; Jan Holm/Loop Images 156 a; Jeff J Mitchell 75 b; Jim Henderson 137; Jiri Rezac 165 a; John Paul 60, 63 a&b, 199 a&b; Hemis 218 b; Matthew Richardson 34; Peter Horee: 17 c; pictureditor 144 a; Scottish Viewpoint: Dennis Hardley 198; Simon Grosset 165 b, 219 r; Stephen Finn 219 l, 241; Universal Images Group/DeAgostini 155, 213; The Wickerman Photography 232 a

Spirit of Place

Text © Charles MacLean 2015
Commissioned images © Allan MacDonald and Lara Platman 2015, additional material as specified above.

Charles MacLean has asserted his right to be identified as the author of this work in accordance with the Copyright, Designs and Patents Act 1988 (UK).

Published in 2017 by Frances Lincoln,
an imprint of The Quarto Group,
The Old Brewery, 6 Blundell Street,
London N7 9BH, United Kingdom.
T (0)20 7700 6700 F (0)20 77008066
www.QuartoKnows.com

First Frances Lincoln edition 2015
Second edition 2017

A catalogue record for this book is available from the British Library.

ISBN 978-0-7112-3891-6

Printed and bound in China

Produced for Frances Lincoln by Tracy Killick Art Direction and Design and www.editorsonline.org

Project Editor: Sarah Tomley
Art Director: Tracy Killick
Proofreader: Louise Abbott
Indexer: Hilary Bird
Map illustrations: Peter Liddiard at Sudden Impact Media

Brimming with creative inspiration, how-to projects and useful information to enrich your everyday life, Quarto Knows is a favourite destination for those pursuing their interests and passions. Visit our site and dig deeper with our books into your area of interest: Quarto Creates, Quarto Cooks, Quarto Homes, Quarto Lives, Quarto Drives, Quarto Explores, Quarto Gifts, or Quarto Kids.

MIX
Paper from responsible sources
FSC® C008047